THE WORLD'S YOUR STAGE

THE WORLD'S YOUR STAGE

How Performing Artists Can Make a Living
While Still Doing What They Love

WILLIAM F. BAKER | WARREN C. GIBSON
EVAN LEATHERWOOD

AMACOM

AMERICAN MANAGEMENT ASSOCIATION

New York · Atlanta · Brussels · Chicago · Mexico City · San Francisco
Shanghai · Tokyo · Toronto · Washington, D.C.

Bulk discounts available. For details visit: www.amacombooks.org/go/specialsales
Or contact special sales: Phone: 800-250-5308 Email: specialsls@amanet.org
View all the AMACOM titles at: www.amacombooks.org
American Management Association: www.amanet.org

Library of Congress Cataloging-in-Publication Data
Baker, William F., 1942–
The world's your stage : how performing artists can make a living while still doing what they love / William F. Baker, Warren C. Gibson, and Evan Leatherwood.
pages cm
Includes bibliographical references and index.
ISBN 978-0-8144-3615-8 (pbk.) -- ISBN 978-0-8144-3616-5 (ebook)
1. Performing arts--Vocational guidance. 2. Performing arts--Economic aspects. I. Gibson, Warren C. II. Leatherwood, Evan. III. Title.
PN1580.B35 2015
791.023--dc23   2015029949

About AMA

American Management Association (www.amanet.org) is a world leader in talent development, advancing the skills of individuals to drive business success. Our mission is to support the goals of individuals and organizations through a complete range of products and services, including classroom and virtual seminars, webcasts, webinars, podcasts, conferences, corporate and government solutions, business books, and research. AMA's approach to improving performance combines experiential learning—learning through doing—with opportunities for ongoing professional growth at every step of one's career journey.

Printing number

10 9 8 7 6 5 4 3 2 1

With Gratitude
for Their Ongoing Support

Bernard & Irene Schwartz Foundation
Stephen & Anna-Maria Kellen Foundation
Barbara Slifka
Daniel L. Ritchie
The Robert and Mercedes Eichholz Foundation
James & Frances Berger

CONTENTS

PREFACE

by William F. Baker

WHY WE WROTE THIS BOOK

In my first year of teaching a business course at New York's Juilliard School of dance, drama, and music, I asked one of my students, a gifted pianist whom I'll call Alicia, what she would like to do with her life.

"All I want to do is play the piano before a respectful audience," she answered.

I believe deeply in Alicia's goal, or else I wouldn't have coauthored this book. I also believe, as do my two coauthors, that today's classical performing artists deserve a wide and appreciative audience. But in order for that to be true, I know that Alicia and her peers in music, dance, and theater have to think differently about their work in order to succeed. Just being good at their respective art forms isn't enough. Today's performing artists have to ask a wider range of questions than they are accustomed to asking, and they have to be willing to learn new skills if they want successful careers. These questions and these skills are more commonly associated with business than they are with art.

So in reply I asked Alicia, "How about money? How about getting paid to do that?" Alicia said she didn't really care about that kind of thing. "What about paying the rent? Or paying for food? Is eating something you need to do?" I asked.

It was at that moment that it hit home for Alicia. If she wanted piano performance to be her career and not just a hobby, she would have to figure out how to get paid. Even as their art demands their total concentration, sooner or later all serious young performers must pay attention to this unavoidable reality. This has never been more important than in today's world, where—because of shifting tastes and a digitizing economy—it has become increasingly difficult for the Alicias of the world to establish a financial foundation for their artistic careers.

Recently, 700 dancers—all of them excellent—showed up to audition for a single open position at a New York dance company. Those odds are not just daunting but potentially heartbreaking. Dancers have to make it before they turn 35 and their bodies begin to wear out. How many of those 700 will ever get the chance to dance professionally? More important, how many of those 700 will miss their chance because they were waiting for it to come along rather than taking the initiative to make it happen themselves?

I mention all this not to depress you but to remind you that when we talk about the economics of the performing arts, we aren't just talking about abstract numbers. We are talking about whether people like you will get a chance to pursue their calling over the course of their lives. In this book, we intend to put every tool we can think of in your hands to enable you to make your performing career a reality.

Musicians and actors have more time to make it professionally than dancers do, but their odds are equally unsettling. Fewer symphonies are hiring, and many of them are struggling just to stay alive. Conservatories in the United States graduate about 150,000 musicians each year, even though symphonies have only about 150 open slots per year. Audiences for classical music are shrinking, and so are recording profits. Competition among even the most gifted performers is more intense than ever.

Meanwhile, acting schools are graduating hundreds of talented actors each year even with very few paying roles available on the stage, on television, and in the movies. And, as with music, live audiences for serious theater are tougher and tougher to find.

So what is a performer in the 21st century to do? In 2009, I was approached by Dr. Joseph Polisi, the president of Juilliard, and Fr. Joseph McShane, the president of New York City's Fordham University, which boasts its own highly regarded performing arts program. They asked me to create a course to help give their students—who are among the most gifted in the world—some guidance to help them kick-start their careers. After many years managing media businesses associated with the fine arts, I expected this to be a relatively easy task. Then I sat down to write the syllabus. I thought, *Where do I start?* How *can* a brilliant performer make it against such odds? I really didn't know.

But I got a lot of help from successful friends—the heads of some of the greatest performing arts institutions in the world, many of them located in New York City itself. They have been generous enough to come speak to my students each year, and you will see some of them profiled later in this book. They are men and women of great achievement who care deeply about keeping the flame of great performance burning. After a few years of teaching the class, I saw some of my former students get traction in their careers, and I invited them to come back and offer my students their insights. They talked about the choices they had made and the pitfalls they had encountered on their way to their first real-world success. You will read about some of them later in this book, too.

Teaching this class has not been easy, and I continue to learn so much from my guest lecturers and my students. I am gratified that I have been able to help my students overcome obstacles and inertia and begin careers that show real promise. The class, "Understanding the

Profession: The Performing Arts in the 21st Century," has become a real calling for me. It is the arts, I feel, that are the essence of our humanity and that set us apart from all the other living beings on earth. Cardinal Roger Mahoney, a friend and the former archbishop of Los Angeles, once told me that the arts are one of the very best ways he knew to get close to the divine. I would agree. For everyone, I think, including those who don't identify with a particular religious tradition, the arts link us to the most transcendent parts of ourselves.

In writing this book, I am fortunate to have two colleagues who were willing and able to help take this book from vision to reality. Dr. Warren Gibson, my oldest friend, is an engineer, economist, and sometime amateur musician and classical music buff. Warren believes that if any mortal ever had a direct line to God, it was Johann Sebastian Bach. Evan Leatherwood is a former semiprofessional singer, a journalist, and a Slifka Fellow at Fordham University's Bernard L. Schwartz Center for Media, Public Policy, and Education. He has sat in on my class for the last few years and is happy to help bring its insights to a wider audience.

This book is our guide to the business aspects of the performing arts today. The subject is complex and nuanced. You won't find any formulas for surefire success here, because no such formulas exist. But we hope you will find a pool of wisdom and useful information that will make you stronger and greatly improve your chances of success. In arming you with insight and new ways of thinking about your career, we will draw from many sources: the psychology of salesmanship, the art of working with others, marketing strategies, a firm belief in the importance of kindness (it means a great deal), and some other basic and not-so-basic business and management concepts.

Business is not a dirty word, as many of my students first thought. They came to realize, as I hope you will, that the traditional sources of external career support—commercial profits, philanthropic and government donations—are not the only way forward, and that individually acquired business skills—like reading financial statements, creating business plans, and most important, cultivating an entrepreneurial attitude—can make all the difference in the world.

The digital economy of the 21st century has empowered individuals more than ever before to chart their own economic futures. It has also made individuals more personally responsible than ever before for the prospect of their own success. The power is now truly in your hands as an artist. This book will give you guidance on how to use that power.

HOW TO READ THIS BOOK

Here is a guide to the chapters that follow, so you can locate the specific information you need at this moment in your career. You don't have to read this book in order or in its entirety to get the full benefit from it. But if you do choose to read it from cover to cover, you will be encountering the information in roughly the same order that I present it to my students throughout the semester.

Chapter 1 raises some of the most important questions you can ask yourself as a performer embarking on a new career. Think of it as a continuation of the questions I asked Alicia. Chapter 1 also introduces a few bedrock business concepts that we think can inform your reading of the entire book.

The challenges that face today's performers are unprecedented in some ways. Still, we believe a little understanding of the hurdles that composers and performers of the last three centuries faced and overcame can provide hope and inspiration to today's performers. To that end, we present some examples in Chapter 2, drawn from the lives of eight greats, from Johann Sebastian Bach to the great modern opera singer Beverly Sills.

Chapter 3 is designed to give you an economic snapshot of the performing arts in America as the industry looks today. It is common for people going into other fields, like law, banking, and business, to take a look at their chosen industry before deciding whether it's a good prospect or a good fit for them. But we have found, to our dismay, that this simple bit of preparation is not common for those going into the arts. We hope this chapter will be a first step for you in this kind of preparation. Even just a little understanding of how the industry works can give you a competitive advantage over those who focus exclusively on their craft, oblivious to the bigger picture. So please pay attention to the industry statistics we present. They are broad and general and can seem daunting. But remember, you are more than a statistic. You have talent, and if you stick with us throughout these pages, you will have the beginnings of an understanding of the business of the performing arts. Knowledge is power. That power can give you an edge in a highly competitive environment—so use it!

In Chapter 4, we offer some information about the ongoing digitization of music and, increasingly, other art forms. If we could look into a crystal ball and tell you how best to make a living online as an artist ten years, five years, or even one year from now, trust us—we would do it. In our extensive research of this topic, we have found no expert anywhere, no matter how credentialed, who really has a grasp on what the future holds. So we think that the best strategy is to understand the major technological changes that have brought us to the present moment. To have any hope of understanding where we're headed, we have to know where we've come from, and that's what we offer in Chapter 4.

Chapter 5 is about reading and understanding financial statements. In all the years I've taught "Understanding the Profession," my students, many of them brilliant performers, have been initially afraid of learning the numbers but also incredibly proud of themselves when they did. Those of you who go on to found your own organizations will have no choice but to learn how to understand financial statements. Those of you who go on to work for existing organizations, from symphonies to small ensembles, will want to be able to take a look at the financial health of the places where you're signing on, if only to make sure you'll still have a place to work in the near future!

Chapters 6 and 7 give you a front-row seat in my class, as well as a behind-the-scenes look at some of New York's most prominent and dynamic performing arts institutions. Chapter 6 profiles the managers of some of New York's iconic performing arts organizations, like Peter Gelb, general manager of the Metropolitan Opera, and Sir Clive Gillinson, director of Carnegie Hall. Chapter 7 profiles what we call *artist-entrepreneurs*, younger men and woman who have founded innovative smaller groups that we believe represent the future of the performing arts. These *artist-entrepreneurs* include Claire Chase, CEO, cofounder, and artistic director of the International Contemporary Ensemble, and Max Hodges, who took the fledgling dance company Gallim on a path of rapid and astonishing growth. The material we present in these chapters, which you cannot find anywhere else, is drawn both from one-on-one interviews with these leaders and from their lectures to my class. We asked all of them how they succeeded in their own careers, and we pass their best answers along to you. As we said above, there is no such thing as a surefire formula for success, but we hope that a sampling of the wisdom and experience of the luminaries of the moment might give you that one piece of information or that one insight that will show you your way forward.

Chapter 8 will give you a tour of that most essential skill: raising money. If there is a secret ingredient to success in the performing arts, fundraising is it! All not-for-profits rely on the goodwill and enthusiasm of donors, both those who give large amounts and those who give what they can. I've taken the best insights from my 20 years as head of New York's PBS station, which relied on both kinds of donations, and distilled them here. I also managed to convince Larry Lynn, one of the greatest fundraisers I've ever known, to give you his take on the subject. We've also tossed in some good fundraising advice from other old pros. It's impossible to have too much guidance on this crucial topic.

Chapter 9, covering auditions and agents, will be especially useful to actors but, like the rest of the book, it applies to performers of all types. We start by telling you how to overcome some common blocks to auditioning. Auditioning does not have to be scary, but it does have to be an essential part of every performer's working life. Next up, we unravel the mystery of how to get and work with agents, with advice from two of the best in the business, Paula Poeta and Dustin Flores of the New York–based talent agency The Mine. Chapter 9 ends with the story of my own daughter, Angela, who made it all the way to Broadway before choosing another career. Many actors may follow that route, and there is nothing wrong with it. Being trained as a disciplined performer is an asset in any profession.

Chapter 10 offers some parting words of encouragement. Business can seem like a mundane, even depressing, subject, so we wanted to make sure to remind you why we're all in the arts: It is a sure path to a more meaningful life. And it is an inexhaustible source of surprise, excitement, and joy. We also offer some essential pieces of advice gleaned from the rest of the book. If, in your future career, you find yourself stuck, it's our hope that you can always turn to Chapter 10 and get a quick nudge in the right direction. Running any business is sometimes a slog, but only in the arts is there also magic. Keep that in mind, and you will be up to any challenge.

★ ★ KEYNOTES ★ ★

Actors get notes, musicians play them, and students take them. The students in the class this book is based on are required to turn in one page of notes at the end of each session, summarizing what they've learned.

In that spirit, we're giving you Keynotes at the end of each chapter. They will help you take the information offered and turn it into practical advice that you can start applying to your career today. This book would be remiss if it sought only to inform. We also want to give insight into the very next decision you might have to make. So in each chapter, look at the Keynotes for ways to take what you've learned and apply it directly to your life.

Each Keynotes section has three parts:

1. **Questions to Ask Yourself**
   - Answering these questions will give you insight into where you are and where you're headed, and help you make the material your own by relating it to your specific career goals.

2. **Tips**
   - These are essential pieces of advice, extracted from the chapter.

3. **Exercises**
   - These activities will get you out of your comfort zone, trying new things, and taking one small step at a time to advance your career.

SOME QUESTIONS AND CONCEPTS TO GET YOU STARTED

As Sir Clive Gillinson, the director of New York City's Carnegie Hall, says, sometimes when you're at a loss for answers it is because you are not asking the right questions. Simply ask new questions, and instead of a problem you'll see new paths forward. In that spirit, this chapter presents some questions you might not have thought to ask yourself yet, along with some helpful answers.

A FEW IMPORTANT QUESTIONS

These questions are geared toward performers who want to start their own organizations, those who are coming to be called *artist-entrepreneurs*. The more traditional routes are still there for actors, musicians, and dancers, but at least for the moment, there are fewer of those jobs and the pay is lower than in the past. That doesn't mean you should not consider those traditional routes! But the whole idea of this book is to entice you toward creative experimentation—trying out as many options as you can until you find something that works. In addition to regular career paths, entrepreneurship is being embraced by more and more successful young performing artists as a powerful way of advancing or augmenting their careers.

THE BIG QUESTION

By far the most important question to ask is: "Why are you going into the performing arts business?"

What are you planning to do that's unique and special?

You can't just say, "I just want to play, act, or dance." Your plan can start with that desire, but it has to evolve into more. For example, one of my students, Alex Lipowski (see Chapter 7), was a percussionist at Juilliard. In the course of his academic career, he saw that there was an unmet need for an ensemble to perform experimental new percussion music. So he and a friend organized a group of talented, like-minded performers who began to work together outside of class. They found that people enjoyed not just the music but also the spectacle of a bunch of percussionists whaling away on their drums and appropriated percussion instruments, like discarded car parts and Tibetan singing bowls. As time went on, Alex's supporters organized themselves and donated funds to help support the work, and the Talea Ensemble was born. Talea now performs at venues worldwide and receives contributions from individuals and foundations to help pay the performers.

Alex is an example of real success in a very narrow niche of the performance world. What started as a general love of percussion grew into a specific passion for new music for nontraditional instruments. Connecting with a very narrow but passionate audience like Talea's is one secret to success. Alex had a passion, discovered a niche, developed a plan to fill that niche, and executed it well.

It is critical that you be on the lookout for *exactly* what your business will do and why it's different. Developing the concept may take as much creativity as all the rest of your work. You will need to pursue your broader interests, try out a variety of ideas, and be open to both success and failure. To help clarify what your future business will be, start by asking yourself the questions that follow.

WHO MIGHT MY COMPETITORS BE?

If the product (it can sometimes be clarifying to think of music, dance, or live theater as a product) you want to provide is already being supplied to your community (for example, by an orchestra, a chamber ensemble, or a ballet company), you might have a problem. Why would you want to start a business that supplies a product already supplied by others? Sometimes, there can be good reasons, such as thinking you can do it better or knowing that you have a different approach. You might be able to provide a version of the art that more established groups are not providing or are not interested in or capable of providing. If there is only one large theater venue in your town that mostly sells tickets to commercial touring companies for a high price point, for example, think about how your efforts might be a counterpoint to that. Perhaps a smaller venue and less commercial offerings would find an audience.

We don't mention the idea of competition to frighten you but to nudge you toward strategic thinking. Asking where your work might fit into the marketplace can be a powerful way to give a more concrete shape to your future plans. (For more on this way of thinking, take a look at our discussion of branding in Chapter 6.)

IS THERE A NEED FOR WHAT I PLAN TO DO?

This question may seem too commercial for an artistic undertaking, but it must be considered. If you plan to provide an art for which there is no demand, you have a problem, at least initially. The people in your potential market might not share your passion for early choral music, experimental improv theater, or contemporary dance, and so they might not want to support it financially. This is where your passion meets your evolving business sense. Once you've got something produced that you can show people, don't be afraid to promote it. Thinking like a salesperson in the not-for-profit arts world simply means persistently communicating your own passion for what you do. It does not have to be an inauthentic process. The context might be uncomfortable at first (for example, delivering your message to donors at an event rather than to friends and colleagues informally), but the action is essentially the same. Ask yourself if the world needs what you want to create. If the answer is yes, remember that the world may still need some convincing. And a sense of need is crucial to generating financial support for your art.

You might feel that you don't need much money to support your art, but you'd be surprised how much it costs even to make the most modest artistic venture work. The costs add up quickly: rent, food, travel—you name it. Performers often take support jobs in offices, restaurants, catering, or what have you to provide some income until their artistic work can support them. The rub here is that the degree of artistic success that can liberate you from your office or restaurant job may be a long time coming. Meanwhile, that work can grind you down unless you keep reminding yourself that you're doing it to further your long-term goal.

FOR PROFIT OR NOT?

Should your business be for-profit or not-for-profit? What do you need to start a business?

Both for-profit and not-for-profit organizations bring their own advantages and disadvantages. A for-profit business tends to give you much more control and allows you to keep any profits you may earn. Keep in mind that in the performing arts, "may earn" is a huge qualifier. The serious arts tend to make little money and are often, as you will see, dependent on the generosity and philanthropy of supporters and friends. The performing arts businesses best suited to the for-profit model tend to be popular music groups, Broadway, and some arts support organizations. Film and television are often great for-profit choices for actors. But the decision of for-profit or not-for-profit is yours and must be carefully studied. Remember too that you need resources (money) just to get any business going. You will probably need to incorporate (at a cost of $1,000 or more), amass funds to pay performers, and advertise. Other mandatory and potentially costly activities include building and maintaining a compelling website and arranging transportation to gigs and for tours. Anyone who supports you (i.e., gives you money) in the for-profit model is called an investor, and investors expect a return (a payback of the investment, plus profits). Building a successful for-profit arts business is probably more difficult than you can imagine. But if you think your business might work as a moneymaker, go for it. In the end, owning a business that one can sell or monetize is always good.

If you are a musician or dancer, you will more likely be forming a not-for-profit business. Even the biggest and most successful fine performing arts organizations all tend to be nonprofit. Why? Because these companies need philanthropy. Donations are not made to for-profit businesses, which only accept investments. Not-for-profit businesses accept money from individuals, foundations, and corporations, and if the business is registered as a tax-exempt 501(c)(3) charity, those donors can get a tax deduction for their contributions. Also, as a tax-exempt charity, you may be able to get some services, such as legal work or office space, donated by caring professionals.

BEDROCK CONCEPTS

In addition to the important questions we've just asked, we want to lay down some bedrock pieces of advice that come up again and again from the most high-functioning people we know in the performing arts world.

DON'T QUIT YOUR DAY JOB!

That phrase has been used as a coded way of saying that a performer's work isn't up to snuff—as in "Don't quit your day job because your art isn't going to support you." But we mean it in a more positive sense.

There are huge benefits to a day job. It provides income, financial support, health insurance, daily structure, and a network of friends and colleagues, even if it has nothing at all to do with the performing arts. Those forms of support can be essential to your mental and physical health in the long term as you take up the heroic but extremely difficult work of pursuing a life in the arts. If you're reading this book, you've got your eyes on the prize: a full-time artistic career. That's a good thing! But before your art becomes your full-time work, it's likely to be your part-time work. For many, their art never generates enough income to eliminate the need for a 9 to 5 job. This doesn't need to be a source of shame or cause for a sense of failure. Working on your art along with another career has many fulfilling aspects in its own right.

Most jobs don't allow the freedom to take time off for auditions, performances, and rehearsals, but it's worth it to find one that does. For example, we've seen some success among artists who use their elegance and style to do sales work or nonprofit development. That can be a nice fit. Bethany Heinrich, a Juilliard theater grad, was moved by her mother's cancer recovery to form Fabulous & Fighting, a not-for-profit that takes clothes donated by fashion houses and gives them to women whose cancer treatments are changing the size of their bodies. It turns out that having nice clothes helps a great deal with recovery by bolstering self-image. Bethany found it easy to get clothing manufacturers to contribute to her mission. Starting from scratch, she hosted a gala benefit, raised money, and promoted her idea. She got cancer hospitals to provide space for the clothing that was donated to patients. Her success with Fabulous & Fighting landed her a job in the development department of a landmark New York cultural institution. There, she made more contacts with wealthy, philanthropic-minded people. Now she's earning a living in her secondary career, having fun, achieving personal growth, amassing experience, and doing good to boot. Yet there is enough flexibility in her new career to allow time for her to practice the craft of acting that she mastered at Juilliard and to go to auditions and workshops.

Give your utmost to making a living from your art, but realize that doing it full-time is not the only honorable way of using your talents.

TAP INTO THE POWER OF KINDNESS

A growing amount of new research and a number of recent management books are demonstrating the power of kindness and generosity (including our own *Leading with Kindness*, cowritten with Michael O'Malley [Amacom, 2008]). As Allentown Symphony conductor Diane Wittry says about auditioning new talent, "I'm choosing from a group of people who are all equally talented, so I have to look beyond skill. Whom do I pick? I pick someone I think I'd like to work with. Somebody who's nice." Diane said she would even sacrifice a little talent to have a more compatible person in her orchestra and on her team. We've seen it time and again. People help people they like, often selflessly. In the end, kind people finish first, even if it might not seem like it in the short term. If you spend your career cultivating a network of colleagues whose work you believe in and whose friendship you come to value, you will not arrive at the end of it without accomplishment. As Rabbi Abraham Joshua Heschel said, "When I was young, I valued clever people. Now that I'm old, I value kind people."

DON'T BE AFRAID TO WALK THE INDIRECT PATH

You may clearly know your goal, and it is best to have a clear one in mind, but the way to that goal will likely be indirect.

Right out of school, you might be skilled and fortunate enough to land a job in a major, successful company (be it an orchestra, dance company, or theater), but that's getting less likely, no matter how good your chops. Why? There are probably many good performers out there whose talent is equal to or even greater than yours. In business we call these people "competitors." Competition is good. It raises the stakes for everyone and it makes you and everyone else in your profession strive harder. But it also makes the direct path steeper. The solution? Look for an indirect path.

I have a saying, "When you see an opening, go through it." It means that you have to become *opportunistic* in the best sense of the word, as in willing to see and then grasp an opportunity. A given opportunity may not be what you were hoping for in the end, but if it is honorable, pays money, and gives you new skills and a new network of people, then it will have been well worth your time. So when you see a potential opportunity, don't hold back, and don't overthink it. Just do it and see what happens.

This might sound scary, especially to the musicians out there, who have spent their entire lives mastering a single skill and who are used to progressing down predefined paths past predefined markers of success. But being open to new, unplanned work is essential to navigating the world outside of school. You will have to make many such unplanned decisions and moves in your career. Don't expect every job that you have to be better than the last. You might find yourself going from giving voice lessons to waiting tables before you get your first paying performance gig, for example. Don't see every setback as final or as a judgment of your worth as a person. And be prepared to go in some directions that might feel crazy at the time but which will make sense later. Keep your eyes on your ultimate goal, and the small deviations won't throw you off course.

NETWORKING IS CRITICAL
(OR, YOU CAN'T GO IT SOLO, EVEN AS A SOLOIST)

Anybody who has acted in a company or danced or acted in an ensemble already knows this! You can't make great things alone.

Everybody stresses the importance of networking, but how do you do it? Begin by recognizing that there are often people of means who love your kind of performance and would be willing to help support your efforts. Finding such a person or persons can be the biggest secret to a quick success. But again, how do you do that? Fundraising is one way, which we discuss in Chapter 8. But there's another kind of networking that is critical: the associates you need to make your performance a success.

Even in the case of a solo recital, where you are the only person performing, critical support is still needed. Someone has to find a venue, select a program, deal with wardrobe, promote the event, and do a thousand other things. Some of these elements require top-tier professional support. Over the course of your career, you will develop friends who can help. During your last years at school, while touring, in your various jobs, and while socializing, be sure to keep your eyes out for people who can help you make your magic happen, and whom you can support in return. Trust us, they're out there, just waiting to be asked. We've found that people who are reliable and are "givers" make the best associates and increase your chances for success—not to mention their own as well.

STRIVE FOR AUTHENTICITY

Authenticity is *the* big word these days in the fields of organizational behavior and industrial psychology, and for good reason. Authenticity means being real and true to who and what you are, not pretending. Authentic people admit their failings and know their strengths. They are who they are both to themselves and to others, and in a variety of contexts from home to the workplace. The ability to be authentic arises out of the basic fact that they are comfortable in their own skin. Authentic people have a positive view of themselves and others, and they instinctively extend that positive view in the form of professional trust and offers of support. They are confident in their abilities, but not arrogant. They are usually givers and are willing to selflessly help others.

Being authentic doesn't mean ignoring the rules of politeness or realizing that different social situations can call for different forms of behavior. But it does mean connecting whatever you're doing, from fundraising to rehearsing, in some way to what you believe is worth your time and what you truly value. When people see that whatever you're doing is deeply rooted in what you believe, they will be drawn to your cause.

It's amazing how many people are authentic. You have to be genuine to truly succeed, and surrounding yourself with other genuine people only makes you better. Being authentic is not always easy. You have to be willing to freely share your time and talents with others who can benefit from your skill—not with the expectation that they will help you someday, but because you care about making the world a better place. Sometimes being authentic means passing up certain opportunities or relationships because they don't feel right or because they go against your core beliefs.

Shakespeare said it best, when he had Polonius say to Laertes: "This above all: to thine own self be true/And it must follow, as the night the day/Thou canst not then be false to any man."

DIG DEEP

To get you through the hard parts of your career, remember: It's all part of the adventure. There will be turns of fortune both good and bad. Along the way, you will be doing and learning things that will push you out of your comfort zone and disrupt the very linear ways of thinking you needed to master your conservatory or school training. Don't worry! All emerging artists have felt this way. Remember that you are a creative person at heart and that your creativity is your greatest asset, even and *especially* in your business affairs. This may be hard to believe, but business and management require a great deal of creativity. Managing people and creating a network of professional relationships will draw from your deepest reserves of creative energy as surely as any performance. Embrace the business aspects of your career as an integral part of your identity as an artist, not something in opposition to it. Be grateful for the ways in which the business aspects of your career can help you grow stronger. But they will help you grow stronger only if you are willing to give yourself to them completely and let them transform you for the better. Dig deep, and you will find greater reserves of ingenuity and resiliency than you ever thought were there!

★ ★ **KEYNOTES** ★ ★

Questions to Ask Yourself

- What am I planning to do that's different from the rest of my peers? What special interests, talents, or ideas do I bring to the table as a performer or as an entrepreneur? (If you're not sure, ask your trusted friends, teachers, or a mentor this question. Sometimes we need the perspective of an outsider to appreciate what is exceptional or unique about us.)

- Is anybody in my peer group already doing something interesting and entrepreneurial? If so, do they need help? Are there any established performing arts institutions in my community already doing what I want to do? How can I differentiate myself from them?

Tips

- Don't be afraid of getting a full-time job and pursuing your art at the same time. Especially at the start of your career, there is no shame in banking on the security, structure, and community that a working environment can give you.
- Kindness isn't the same thing as weakness. In fact, it's the exact opposite. Only people who are truly secure in their identity as artists have the capacity to treat everybody, including their direct competitors, with respect. When encountering a rival or a new colleague, go out of your way to be kind. You will never regret it.

Exercises

- If your school has a career services office, go and talk to the staff there and ask if there are any alumni working in your area whom you could contact for advice or potential work. LinkedIn and other online networking services can be great, but they are no replacement for asking a human being with specialized knowledge of your school's alumni network. Plus, getting on the radar of your career services office can be beneficial. You want the staff to have you in mind when that job, scholarship, or residency that is a perfect fit for you comes across their desks.
- Write down a list of 15 people you know who can help you advance your career. They can be teachers, fellow students with similar ambitions, or anybody working in the business of the performing arts. Can't think of 15 people? Then it is time to get out there and circulate and expand your network. Look for people you can help out or

just get to know. You don't have to ask for a favor or give one right away. Remember, effective networking has to be about two things: an authentic desire to help and be helped, and the realization that you're in it for the long haul. Just try to make a real connection at first, and go from there.

STRUGGLES AND TRIUMPHS OF WESTERN MUSICIANS

Performing artists have always had to struggle to make a living. In this chapter, we offer vignettes from the lives of some of the great masters of Western music, from Johann Sebastian Bach to Beverly Sills. It is amazing that these composers and performers were able to achieve so much in the face of obstacles that—though each unique in its own way—were surely no less daunting than those of our time. The examples of these artists may help you develop your own strategy that also combines vision, determination, and clear-eyed confrontation of hard facts.

JOHANN SEBASTIAN BACH:
JANITOR, TEACHER, FATHER OF 20

Johann Sebastian Bach (1685–1750) was born into a family of musicians. Inherited talent and his father's teaching gave him a fast start on his life of music. In 1700, he turned 15, which in those days meant entry into adulthood. Both of his parents had died, and one of his younger brothers had already entered an apprenticeship—a reminder to Johann Sebastian, if he needed one, of his obligation. It was time to go out into the world.

Rather than follow his brother's footsteps into apprenticeship, Bach decided—on his own initiative, as far as we know—to apply for a scholarship at the prestigious St. Michael's School in Lüneberg. He got one. Music was his passion, but he also studied the usual subjects of the time there: logic, rhetoric, Greek, and Latin. In return for room, board, and tuition, he was required to sing for church services, weddings, funerals, and such, but only as long as he remained a boy soprano. Nature took its course more slowly in those days than it does now, and he kept his soprano voice almost to the age of 17. There is no indication that he was a candidate for castration, a practice that was still very much in vogue at that time, as male sopranos were thought to be superior to females. Lucky for Bach; lucky for us! Had he succumbed to the knife, he would not have bequeathed to us two sons who also rose to the top ranks of composers. Bach stayed on as an ex-soprano at St. Michael's for a short time as an instrumental player, but soon after that he had to go.

The credentials he earned at St. Michael's did not guarantee employment. Opportunities for musicians were limited; a position with an aristocratic patron was almost the only avenue open to a talented musician in 1703. Bach worked for Duke Johann Ernst in Weimar as an organist, then as *Konzertmeister* (orchestra leader). His duties went beyond music and may even have included some janitorial tasks! When the position of *Kapellmeister* (head of all musical activities) became available, Bach applied for it, but a rival got it instead. Bach submitted his resignation, and for his impertinence, he was imprisoned for four weeks before being released from the duke's service.

History does not record whether Bach, emerging from his jail cell, wondered if he should just give it all up. We do know that he found another position in short order because his reputation as an exceptionally talented organist had gotten around. Thereafter, he held a succession of church positions under the patronage of various dukes and princes, none of them far from Leipzig. None of these positions were sinecures; throughout most of his life, he had to steal time for composing from his busy teaching and conducting schedule.

If Bach had produced only one work in his lifetime—say, the glorious *Mass in B Minor*—he would have earned his place as a pillar of Western music. That he could pour out so many excellent works for organ, keyboard, and chorus, all of which have stood the test of time, is well-nigh incomprehensible when we consider not only his daily chores but also his role as husband and father. His first wife bore him seven children (only three of whom survived childhood), and following her death, a second wife bore him 13 more!

Bach's life span coincided roughly with the Age of Enlightenment. The power of the Church was declining as reason began to ascend. The benefits of specialization and trade were becoming more and more evident, and a bourgeois merchant class took shape. Newly able to afford some of the finer things of life, some members of the emerging middle class provided new sources of demand for music and art. The new demand was satisfied less by patronage and increasingly through the gradual emergence of commercial outlets for performances and compositions.

MOZART AND THE HUSTLER

The Internet has revolutionized the performing arts and just about everything else in a mere 20 years. In contrast, the shift from aristocratic toward commercial support for the arts took many decades. The shift didn't happen fast enough to spare Wolfgang Amadeus Mozart (1756–1791) from a lifetime of financial woes. His constant money problems, documented in numerous begging letters sent to wealthy friends, were partly a result of his inability to handle money. But they also reflected the limited opportunities of the time. Although Mozart did secure a number of minor positions, he never had the security that was provided to his contemporary, Joseph Haydn, by his patron, Count Esterházy.

Mozart offered subscription concerts, prepaid by audiences, with varying degrees of success and took pupils, but by the late 1780s, he was in a precarious position. He hoped that an opportunity would open upon the death of Emperor Joseph II in 1790, when it was expected that Joseph's successor, Leopold, would establish his authority by shaking up the court personnel. Indeed, as a result of Joseph's death, Antonio Salieri lost his longtime position as *Kapellmeister*. Mozart practically begged for the position but was rebuffed. He was reduced to soliciting pupils once again.

Even so, this was when he composed some of his finest works. Some consider *The Magic Flute* to be Mozart's greatest opera, yet it was not composed as an opera in the strict sense but rather as a *singspiel*, somewhat akin to a contemporary Broadway musical. It premiered at a suburban music hall, the Theater auf der Wieden in Vienna. The theater's proprietor was Emanuel Schikaneder. George Marek describes him as an "extravagant, irresponsible, capricious Jack-of-all-trades . . . so enthusiastic and so persuasive that few could resist him." Schikaneder played an important role in the writing of *The Magic Flute*. He convinced Mozart, his fellow Freemason, to collaborate on an "easy" comedy with music. He asked Mozart to throw in "all the sure-fire ingredients he knew: magic effects, moral preaching, an evil spirit or two, a comic little Moor . . . trial by fire and water, two pairs of lovers, and for himself, a part [Papageno, the bird catcher] where he could improvise jokes."[1] Mozart reluctantly provided all those gimmicks. But Mozart being Mozart, he produced a work that can be understood on many levels. *The Magic Flute* is a rollicking farce to begin with, a paean to Masonic values, and even more broadly, a stand for Enlightenment ideals versus hidebound tradition. Outright criticism of royalty was dangerous, but (as Dmitri Shostakovich did two centuries later) Mozart landed oblique blows on the ruling class. Audiences of the time, for example, could easily see Empress Maria Theresa in the opera's evil Queen of the Night. Though these topical themes may have faded, the opera's timeless themes of love, compassion, and courage make it an enduring favorite of audiences.

The work was a great success. Schikaneder made (and subsequently lost) a lot of money on it. But not Mozart, who died a few months after its premiere and was buried in a pauper's grave. As for Schikaneder, he died in 1812, insane and penniless.

BEETHOVEN STRIKES A HARD BARGAIN

The production of *The Magic Flute* for a popular audience was a landmark in the shift toward commercial music performance and publication. The trend continued with Ludwig van Beethoven (1770–1827), who derived most of his income from publication royalties, especially after his legendary deafness made subscription concerts impractical. Sometimes, for a fee, he would grant a noble family exclusive rights to a new work for six months or a year, thereafter seeking competitive bids from publishers.[2] He received only a one-time payment from publishers rather than continuing royalties because in the absence of copyright laws, publishers would soon lose their advantage over rival copycat publishers. Income from commissioned works was secondary, and while paid performances provided steady income early in Beethoven's life, that avenue was gradually closed to him by his deafness. Beethoven encountered many difficulties in dealing with various publishers, but he was evidently a skilled negotiator and never had the kind of money problems that Mozart had. In fact, his negotiating tactics extended almost to fraud and deceit. Starting in 1819, he promised his much anticipated mass, the *Missa Solemnis*, to at least six publishers, playing one against the other until a contract was finally signed in 1824.[3]

What of the performers of this era? The households of the nobility maintained large servant staffs, including musicians. The musicians were there to provide background music, not to perform concerts as we think of them. Thus, they really were servants, and their rank in the household was not far above that of the kitchen staff, as evidenced by salary scales of the time. Those pay scales are difficult to compare with modern times because so much of the compensation was provided in kind. Their cash wages were a pittance if they got any at all, but they did receive allowances of food, firewood, candles, and sometimes lodging.

GIUSEPPE VERDI: ITALIAN NATIONALIST HERO

Giuseppe Verdi (1813–1901) is the undisputed king of grand opera. Verdi entered adulthood in the 1830s, a time when the Industrial Revolution and the concomitant spectacular if uneven takeoff of economic growth was well under way. He was born into modest circumstances and benefited greatly from private lessons and opportunities to attend all sorts of musical performances. A teaching position that he secured at the age of 22 led to personal connections with many of the leading figures of the Italian musical scene. He thereby managed to get an opera, *Oberto*, produced at La Scala in Milan. Although *Oberto* was only a modest success, the opera was good enough to land him a contract to produce three more operas for that famous house.

Verdi's contract was offered by Bartolomeo Merelli, La Scala's impresario. The position of impresario evolved along with Italian opera as an example of the specialization and division of labor that are key to economic growth. The process of assembling and scheduling the required actors, musicians, and singers was becoming increasingly complex, so theater owners found it worth their while to hire specialists to handle these chores and, in many cases, to arrange financing as well.

Verdi's career blossomed in parallel with the movement for Italian independence and unification. The chorus "Va pensiero" from his early opera *Nabucco* became an anthem for Italian freedom and is even today sung in that spirit. Verdi became involved in politics himself, and his name became an acronym for a political slogan: "_V_ittorio _E_manuelle, _R_e _d'I_talia"—Victor Emanuel for King of Italy.

Verdi's productive career stretched past age 80. He left behind more than three dozen operas (most of them still performed), a *Requiem Mass*, and miscellaneous vocal and orchestral works. He became quite wealthy, enough so that he could turn to philanthropy himself, founding a home for retired musicians in Milan.[4] His wealth came from the immense popularity of his work and favorable contracts provided by his longtime publisher, the House of Ricordi (or Casa Ricordi), which remains in business to this day. Giovanni Ricordi, the founder of the company, had been instrumental in bringing copyright law to Italy, which gave publishers some assurance that they could recoup high royalty costs from protected future revenues.

LILLIAN NORTON SHOWS TRUE GRIT AND BECOMES MME. NORDICA

Operatic sopranos are a temperamental lot; intense rivalries are not uncommon. So when Clara Louise Kellogg, the great American soprano of the 1870s and 1880s, heaped praise on a young rival, we can be pretty sure she meant it:

> My admiration for Mme. Nordica is deep and abounding. . . . If I wanted any young student to learn by imitation, I could say to her, "Go and hear Nordica and do as nearly like her as you can!" There are not many singers, nor have there ever been many, of whom one could say that. And one of the finest things about this splendid vocalism is that she has had nearly as much to do with it as had God Almighty in the first place.[5]

Giglia Nordica ("Lily of the North") was the mellifluous stage name taken by the young American singer Lillian Norton upon her arrival in Europe, where she soon thrilled opera audiences in Italy and across the Continent. In the last sentence of this quote, Mme. Kellogg is saying that although Mme. Nordica was blessed with prodigious God-given talent, she never would have made it without extraordinary grit and determination.

Lillian Norton (1857–1914) was born in a modest farmhouse in Farmington, Maine. When she was seven, her family moved to Boston to be near the New England Conservatory of Music—not to enroll Lillian but her older sister, Wilhelmina. Lillian would copy Willie as she practiced at home, but she got no training herself until age 14, when, following her sister's untimely death, their mother took Lillian to the Conservatory for evaluation. Wilhelmina's former teacher "was astounded after taking Lillian up the scale and hearing her hit a secure, ringing high C."[6]

Even after her fame had spread, life was a struggle for Mme. Nordica. She drove herself relentlessly not only because of her single-minded ambition but also because her finances were chronically perilous and she was not a quick study. She had no wealthy backer and had to sustain herself and her mother, who accompanied her everywhere. When the time came for her to debut at London's Covent Garden, Mme. Nordica walked from her cheap hotel room to the theater, lacking cab fare. An unfortunate love life made matters worse. Her first husband's "resentment of her singing and hatred of music in general bordered on the psychotic."[7] Two other marriages and various affairs were not much happier.

Still, she soldiered on. At the age of 53, she relearned Isolde in French for a single performance.[8] Once, late in life, she performed all three Brünnhildes on consecutive nights.

GEORGE GERSHWIN CATCHES A WAVE IN THE ALLEY

By 1900, the U.S. economy was booming, thanks to several decades of economic freedom, monetary stability, and a strong work ethic. Immigrants poured into New York City and into housing and working conditions that seem unimaginably harsh from today's perspective. But many families had saved enough that they could splurge on the "home entertainment center" of the time: a piano. "Content delivery" in those days meant a trip to a store or placing a mail order for sheet music or piano rolls for player pianos. Although copyright law protected music in these forms, it was not a deciding factor in the success of the music publishing business simply because copying a piece of sheet music was so tedious. Then, like most other industries, the sheet music business began to consolidate. Consolidation meant larger companies, but it also meant that similar companies tended to gravitate to small areas, sometimes a single street in Manhattan. Such was the case with Tin Pan Alley.

Tin Pan Alley was a block of West 28th Street in Manhattan where a number of music publishers had established their businesses by 1900. The "Tin Pan Alley" appellation, a likely reference to the cacophony of sounds filling the block, was later applied to the music publishing business in general. Jacob Gershvin (or Gershwine, as some sources have it), was the son of immigrants; he brought his talent and drive to the Alley at age 15. He had no trouble finding employment there at $15 per week. Two years later, he pocketed $5 for his first commercial song publication. From that modest beginning, success followed upon success, and he became George Gershwin (1898–1937) along the way. He composed hit songs, Broadway musicals, and later, full-blown symphonic and operatic works. Clearly, Gershwin—and we who love his music—benefited enormously from the commercialization of music, which in turn was a by-product of the rising prosperity into which he was born.

We might add that Gershwin's career paralleled the rise of sound recordings, closely followed by "talking pictures" (movies with sound). We may not think much of this now, but the fact is that sound recording, in its time, was seen by many as a major threat to the performing arts. The first Victrola records were just a scratchy novelty. But those who were looking ahead must have asked themselves what would happen to the demand for live musicians when sound recordings improved to the point where they would be acceptable as substitutes for musicians in theaters, restaurants, churches, and even brothels.

Sound recordings were indeed a "disruptive innovation," to use a contemporary phrase. Some musicians in the aforementioned venues did lose their jobs. But without question, the net effect of sound recording was positive for musicians. As more people gained exposure to music through Victrolas and later their radio receivers, the overall demand for music and other performing arts increased rapidly, and some of that demand was met by live performances. Copyright protection and the licensing schemes promulgated by ASCAP (the American Society of Composers, Authors, and Publishers) and BMI helped protect the incomes of composers and performers whose recorded music was played for public audiences in restaurants or on the radio.

STALIN SCOWLS AND SHOSTAKOVICH SWEATS

In some socialist countries, the arts, like almost everything else, are under government control. Success in these countries depends crucially on developing political skills and currying favor with the ruling elite. Among composers, no example is more vivid than the story of Dmitri Shostakovich (1906–1975), one of the 20th century's greatest symphonic composers. Throughout his rocky career, Shostakovich was torn between his creative urges and a genuine desire to fit into the Soviet system.

In 1936, Soviet leader Joseph Stalin attended a performance of Shostakovich's opera *Lady Macbeth of the Mtsensk District*. Out of the corner of his eye, Shostakovich spotted Stalin responding with derision from his box. Knowing what was coming, and knowing as every Soviet citizen did that crossing Stalin could mean exile to Siberia or death, Shostakovich began to sweat. News of Stalin's displeasure spread quickly, and critics who had praised the opera had to backpedal furiously. For a time, Shostakovich retreated into movie scores, which Stalin liked. Later, his patriotic wartime *Seventh Symphony* returned him to the authorities' good graces. But by 1948, he was in trouble again because the official critics had read anti-Soviet tendencies into his music, as they could do seemingly on a whim. Shostakovich fully expected to be arrested and hauled off to a labor camp. That didn't happen, but with his expulsion from the Music Conservatory, he lost his only source of income. He survived, and with the general easing of Soviet repression following Stalin's 1953 death, Shostakovich gradually recovered his standing with the Communist Party.

No one interpreted Shostakovich better than Leonard Bernstein, who more than anyone else was responsible, mainly through his televised concerts, for introducing Shostakovich to American audiences. Shostakovich lived until 1975, long enough to witness a triumphant performance of his *Fifth Symphony* by the New York Philharmonic, led by Bernstein. We can only hope that unlike some of his forebears, Shostakovich may have died with some inkling that appreciation of his work would continue to grow after he was gone.

BEVERLY SILLS: SINGER, MANAGER, MOM

Beverly Sills (1929–2007) was a popular and talented coloratura soprano. Much has been written about how she maintained a cheerful outlook and built a spectacular operatic career in the face of personal tragedy. Miss Sills once described herself not as a happy person (one who enjoys happy circumstances) but a cheerful person (one who smiles in spite of it all). Her story is of special interest to us not just because of her determination and good cheer but also because of her successful transition from performance to opera management.

Belle Silverman was born in Brooklyn, New York, the daughter of immigrant parents. Her mother was a musician and her father an insurance broker. She was a child prodigy, appearing on radio at age four and winning a prize on the radio program *Major Bowes' Amateur Hour* at ten. In those days, most performers with Jewish names Anglicized them, and so Belle became Beverly Sills. Her career path included the radio program *Arthur Godfrey's Talent Scouts*, Gilbert and Sullivan roles, and light opera. Her first taste of grand opera came in 1947 when she was given a supporting role in *Carmen* for the Philadelphia Civic Grand Opera Company, close to New York geographically but thousands of miles away artistically. Her path from Philadelphia to New York included stops in St. Louis, the Borscht Belt, San Francisco, and many other places. She appeared on a DuMont Television Network program in 1955 that had her not just singing but doing live commercials for salad dressing. She was paid not with cash but with as much of the sponsors' food and wine products as she could carry.[9]

Miss Sills made it to the New York City Opera in 1955. Her debut in *Die Fledermaus* was a hit. She had broken into the New York scene in the company of Cornell MacNeil and other top singers. But the company's $75 performance fee was no solution to her chronic money problems. She continued to perform in obscure venues even after her NYCO debut.

American opera singers often spend considerable time in Europe as students or performers. Miss Sills limited her time abroad because she had two children with special needs and wanted to stay close to them. One child, in a cruel twist of fate, was born deaf. Miss Sills's devotion to her children, and later to the cause of childhood disabilities, constitutes an unusual and inspiring dimension of her life story.

In 1971, *Time* magazine saw fit to name Beverly Sills "America's Queen of Opera" and to feature her on its cover. But her Metropolitan Opera debut came only in 1975, following the departure of the imperious Sir Rudolf Bing as the Met's general director. Of Sir Rudolf, she once said, departing from her typical tactful way, "Oh, Mr. Bing is an ass . . . just an improbable, impossible General Manager of the Metropolitan Opera."[10] They later reconciled.

Opera stars can be just as difficult as general managers, and Sir Rudolf may have seen things differently. But Beverly Sills was not the stereotypical temperamental diva. Her matter-of-fact manner made her a popular guest on television talk shows. For a brief time, she even hosted her own show, which, although confined to a backwater Sunday morning time slot on NBC, won an Emmy Award.

Amazing as it is to see in one person an opera star, wife, mother, and advocate for the disabled, there is more. In her late 40s, Miss Sills began to plan her retirement. This has to be an agonizing time of life for any great singer, whose sole musical instrument resides in her own body. You're at the height of your career, showered with plaudits, making good money. Why even think of giving it all up? But time takes its toll, and Miss Sills wanted to bow out while audiences were still clamoring to see her. She was wise not to linger (as did famed *bel canto* soprano Montserrat Caballé, for example, who continued to perform well into her 70s, her voice dwindling to a shadow of its former self). So in 1978, Miss Sills announced a farewell gala to take place at the New York City Opera in 1980. By that time, she had already given considerable thought to her next career. She transitioned into the position of general director of the NYCO in 1979, even before her gala took place.

No amount of artistic talent or experience is in itself adequate preparation for such a daunting job as opera management. Her background naturally gave Miss Sills good preparation for dealing with principal singers—their temperaments, their agents, and their schedules. But that was just the beginning. Major donors had to be culti-vated and stroked. Union musicians were not shy about pressing their demands. Politicians and bureaucrats required her attention in return for city and state government support, and the same was true of private foundations. The head of a nonprofit organization like the NYCO doesn't just give orders and await results as the CEO of a private firm would expect.[11]

The NYCO prospered during Miss Sills's tenure, which ended in 1989, and continued to prosper under her hand-picked successor. Its budget grew from $9 million to $29 million during her tenure, and she left the company with a surplus.[12] Although challenges continued under her successors, the good times continued up until about 2007, the start of the Great Recession and also the year of Miss Sills's death.

A sad postscript ends our quick look at the life of Beverly Sills. One wonders how well she could have maintained her good cheer had she lived to see the unhappy ending of her beloved New York City Opera. As this was written, the company was dead, having canceled its 2013–2014 season and filed for Chapter 11 bankruptcy. Music critic Anthony Tommasini commented in the *New York Times*:

> [A]rtistic excellence is not enough. Any institution … must have a clear artistic vision, a purpose … the performing arts have never been profit-making endeavors. It is more important than ever that all insti-tutions, from a fledgling string quartet to the lofty Metropolitan Opera, have an effective business model.[13]

★ ★ KEYNOTES ★ ★

Questions to Ask Yourself

- Where do I see myself after my prime performing years are over? Are there elder members of my profession whom I can speak with who can give me advice about long-term career planning? Dancers and singers especially don't have their whole lives to perform. Since their bodies are also their instruments, aging takes those instruments away.

- What are my core values or those of my organization? It can be powerful to clearly articulate in a mission statement what guides you or your organization. Listing "excellence" or "creating transformational artistic experiences" might seem redundant, especially if you have spent many years burrowed in the educational ranks of your particular performing art, where these values are taken for granted. But in the context of the larger world, where a multiplicity of organizations and professions exist, most not devoted to art, having a clear mission statement can remind you why the work you do is special. It can also help guide your day-to-day decision making.

- I know I must make money to make my career work. How about multiple jobs to get me to the target? (Don't put all your eggs in one basket. Having multiple sources of income, especially as a freelancer, is not only a great way to build a strong network but also to insure yourself against danger if one of your sources of income dries up.)

Tips

- Don't waste time regretting that there is no secure economic path for performing artists. As you can see from the lives of Bach, Mozart, Beethoven, Verdi, and the other greats profiled in this chapter, no economic climate in history has made the business career of musicians secure or their path of professional advancement easy to discern. For performers of every age, careers have been full of struggle and improvisation. We believe, of course, that the performing arts are deeply worthy of economic reward, but we also know that obtaining that reward is likely going to be an ever-changing, difficult game. In presenting the lives of these musical greats, we have tried to show you that it has ever been so. So don't waste your vital time and energy regretting it, but accept the conditions of the world and devote all your energies to blazing your own path!

- When you get discouraged (and everybody does), think about what Bach went through, or Mozart or Shostakovich. Listen to a Bach cantata, or the overture to *The Magic Flute*, or Shostakovich's *Seventh*. There's no better way to remind yourself what it's all about.

- Our world is changing rapidly, and you must expect change to continue. Content is increasingly streamed electronically, and compensation avenues are uncertain. But it's almost always the case that when one door closes (or narrows), others open. For example, in the early 20th century, the music business not only survived the advent of sound recording but went on to thrive.

- Remember how fortunate we are to be the beneficiaries of the Enlightenment and the Industrial Revolution. It was only as basic needs were more and more abundantly met that there was excess income and leisure time, some of which went into greater demand for the arts.

- Religious institutions are still reliable places to find musical employment, especially in big cities. Major churches often pay singers and musicians to provide music for their services.

Exercises

- Pick your favorite performing artists, living or dead, and see if they've written an autobiography or if biographies have been written about them. Read the books and see how these artists paid the bills, what their early struggles were, and how they overcame them. If your heroes are living and there are no biographies, look for interviews where they talk about their careers (or even consider getting in touch with them and asking for a meeting—you never know until you try!). You might be surprised to find out that the life of your artistic heroes have more uncertainty, initial failure, or struggle than you thought. Great artists were not born into the world fully formed and on the brink of great achievements. At some point, they were just like you, young people at the start of their careers, full of as-yet-to-be-realized ambitions.

- In order to advance her career, the great opera singer Lillian Norton transformed herself into Mme. Giglia Nordica. A century later, fellow diva Belle Silverman transformed herself into Beverly Sills. Image is crucial to a performer's success, especially when the Internet has put rudimentary marketing tools in the hands of everybody. What to you is a life of endless (even if joyfully undertaken) work might seem to your audience a life of glamour and mystery. Think of some ways you can be innovative and have fun with the image you project to your audience. Think back to the heroic figures who first attracted you to performance. Consider that their public image may have been very different from their day-to-day experience as working members of their profession. Look at successful performers in your peer group and see what sort of image they project. Note what you like and experiment with doing something similar yourself. Note also that while your image is an artificially constructed version of yourself, it has to be rooted at least in part in who you are for it to be truly effective.

THE PERFORMING ARTS AS
AN INDUSTRY

If you are contemplating a career in the performing arts or have already begun one, you should be aware of some basic facts about the performing arts as an industry. This is true of anyone who is interested in a career in a particular area. You need to know how your chosen industry functions. It would be no different if you had a passion for steelmaking, for example. Every aspiring steelmaker should understand that the steel industry is capital-intensive (that is, it requires a great deal of money to produce its products), highly concentrated (with a few large companies), noisy and dirty, technologically mature, and subject to foreign competition. The performing arts business is quite different: It's labor-intensive (that is, it requires a large number of workers or a great amount of work), fragmented (with many small to medium-size organizations), nearly immune from foreign competition, currently buffeted by revolutions in content generation and distribution, and faced with discretionary demand. Products like steel can be sourced from foreign competitors; services like musical performances (or things like haircuts) cannot, save for occasional foreign groups performing on tour. Discretionary demand means that when people are financially pinched, some of the first expenses they jettison are theater tickets or donations to their local symphony. In contrast, a car is a necessity for many of us, which means that demand for steel continues pretty much unabated during hard times. We have to replace our cars when they wear out.

We understand that performing artists live for their art—to play, sing, act, or dance. We also understand that artists tend to banish the world of money and finance to a dark corner of their minds. It needn't be that way and it shouldn't be. Isn't it obvious that artists must make their way and earn a living in this world just like everyone else? And artists must be especially careful not to fall victim to those who would take advantage of them financially. A little time spent learning the business side of the arts can pay off handsomely, laying the groundwork for surviving and prospering as a performing artist. The performing arts are a unique and special calling, to be sure, but one that operates as an industry within the larger economy just like almost all other forms of human activity. Thinking of it this way can be both clarifying and empowering.

To that end, let's look at some basic facts about the performing arts, remembering that this book does not cover popular or mass-media entertainment forms such as rock concerts. We will examine briefly how companies are organized and financed, who supports them (both as audiences and as donors), who is employed, and how they are paid.

PERFORMING ARTS ORGANIZATIONS: NOT-FOR-PROFIT AND FOR-PROFIT

Nearly half of all performing arts companies are organized as either not-for-profit (a.k.a. nonprofit) companies or for-profit corporations. Many people are confused about the differences between the two kinds of organizations. Those differences are not as clear-cut as the labels suggest. The National Football League (whose commissioner's annual compensation is more than $40 million) and the American Automobile Association, for example, are nonprofit organizations, even though they may appear to casual observers to operate just like for-profit companies.

While it is true that nonprofits do not *seek* profits, that doesn't mean they can't *earn* profits, which are an excess of revenues over expenses over the course of a given year. Like profit-oriented companies, nonprofits must avoid sustained losses lest they use up all their reserves and be driven into bankruptcy (relief from debt) or liquidation (dissolution of the organization). The difference is that any profits that a nonprofit earns must be retained in the organization and used to further its mission because there are no shareholders to lay claim to those profits. In contrast, the shareholders of for-profit corporations expect them to earn profits and, at least eventually, provide returns in the form of dividends (surpluses paid to shareholders).

A nonprofit organization must be guided by an explicit public service mission, whereas for-profit companies aim to reward shareholders for risking their savings by investing in the business. For-profit companies may have a mission statement that proclaims a public service mission, but whether they have such a statement or not, competitive forces in free markets exert strong pressure on companies to serve the public, as explained by none other than the father of modern economics, Adam Smith, in his seminal work *The Wealth of Nations*. To earn profits, for-profit companies must attempt to anticipate and satisfy customer demands, be they crass or sublime. In contrast, nonprofits are supposed to educate and lead the public rather than follow the popular whims of the day. The San Francisco Symphony, for example, regularly presents forward-thinking, experimental music and performances with unusual collaborators such as the heavy-metal band Metallica, but the Symphony can't get too far ahead of audiences. To help this medicine go down, the Symphony must also provide plenty of "sugar" from the standard classical repertoire. Heavy-hitting supporters, for the most part, want the classics.

Nonprofit performance organizations rely on donations to cover a large part of their expenses. Ticket sales, even when added to ancillary revenues from food service and gift shops, hardly cover the operating costs of symphony, opera, or dance companies. Nor do ticket sales cover major capital investments like new performance halls. Davies Symphony Hall in San Francisco, for example, where the San Francisco Symphony plays, was financed in large part by a wealthy donor and is owned and operated by the city of San Francisco; the Symphony is a tenant.

Both for-profit and nonprofit organizations are governed by boards of directors. Boards of for-profit companies are at least nominally accountable to shareholders. They are paid for their efforts and are expected to own shares of the company stock. Nonprofit boards are accountable to their donors, to the public at large, and to the Internal Revenue Service, which judges their eligibility for tax breaks. These board members are not compensated and in fact are usually expected to donate generously from their personal funds and often to engage directly in fundraising activities as well.

Nonprofit organizations, provided they meet certain IRS criteria and file the necessary paperwork, are exempt from corporate income tax and (usually) from paying sales taxes on their purchases. More important, donors to nonprofits can deduct their donation amounts from their taxable income.

Further blurring the distinction between the for-profit and nonprofit worlds, large corporations often donate to local arts groups, especially those located in their headquarters city. It is difficult to say whether they are motivated by genuine charitable impulses or by public relations considerations. It is safe to say that most of the time, both motives are at work. A recent program book of the San Francisco

Symphony, for example, shows the Chevron Corporation and Wells Fargo & Company as providers of major long-term funding, with dozens of other corporations and corporate foundations as lesser donors.

Large for-profit corporations typically pay their executives handsomely, but some nonprofits also pay surprisingly well. Thus, a recent IRS filing reported in the *New York Times* revealed that Peter Gelb, the general manager of the Metropolitan Opera, had taken home $1.8 million in pay and benefits in 2012.[1] This disclosure came at an inopportune time, as the Met had been asking its workers to accept reduced pay and benefits. (The Met said Gelb had taken a 10 percent pay cut for 2013.) A salary of this magnitude may rub some donors and ticket buyers the wrong way. On the other hand, the very few individuals who are qualified for such a complex and demanding managerial job as Gelb's can typically earn much more in the for-profit sector. For nonprofits, it is important to be as transparent as possible with compensation decisions.

Not just managers but employees of nonprofits sometimes do very well. The same *New York Times* article mentioned above notes three union stagehands at the Met who, with overtime, took in more than $450,000 in one year. During a brief strike by the San Francisco Symphony players in 2013, it came to light that the average salary there was about $140,000.[2] We do not judge the merit of this figure but simply note that there was little public support for the strike, and it ended soon.

When it comes to worrying about how salaries will be perceived by people both within your organization and outside it, there are two guiding principles: transparency and context. Making it difficult to find out how much people at your nonprofit organization make will likely be seen as an attempt to hide something, which never looks good. People expect nonprofits to be as open and honest as possible about how they operate. If your board has trouble standing by its compensation decisions, it is probably a sign that the board needs to reevaluate them or needs to be prepared to educate the public and the media about the context for those decisions.

INDUSTRY DATA

Some facts and figures can help you understand the performing arts viewed as an industry. We confine our analysis here to the United States and exclude rock concerts and other popular fare.

With a few exceptions, as when major companies go on tour or appear on national television, performing arts organizations serve local, not national, audiences. The result is that the performing arts as an "industry" is highly fragmented. In 2012, the Census Bureau counted 9,073 companies nationwide, 44 percent of them organized as nonprofits.[3] The combined annual revenue of these companies is about $14 billion, which is about one-fifth of the annual revenue of a single commercial media company, Comcast. Of those performing arts companies that operate year-round, about two-thirds generate annual revenues of less than $500,000, about half of what a typical convenience store takes in. One-third of the companies are located in either California or New York, states that account for about 19 percent of the U.S. population.

Nationwide, the Census Bureau counts about 3,000 theater companies, 850 symphonies, 600 dance companies, and 200 opera companies as of 2012. About one-fourth of the dance companies, nearly half of the theater companies, and two-thirds of the musical organizations are nonprofit.

The finances of nonprofit arts groups are of particular interest. As Figure 3-1 shows, earned income (primarily ticket sales but also profits from food service and gift shops) covers, on average, only a little more than half of expenses. Shortfalls are made up from voluntary donations, most of which come from individuals (with some from corporations and foundations) and from government agencies (with roughly equal amounts from local, state, and federal agencies). The "voluntary" nature of individual donations is sometimes stretched to the limit. Subscribers to major symphony orchestras or opera companies, for example, find a "suggested" donation amount added to their bills. Box seats at the major symphony and opera companies come with a hefty and nearly ironclad donation expectation. It's not legally binding, because if it were, it would be part of the ticket price and not a tax-deductible contribution. It's just the thing to do.

Even among commercial, for-profit performance organizations, ticket sales cover only about two-thirds of expenses. These organizations, of course, do not receive donations; the rest of their income comes from ancillary sources such as food service, gift shop receipts, and advertising in program books.

The proportions of revenue earned by nonprofit companies vary considerably. Among dance companies, 85 percent of the revenue is received by nonprofits. For theater companies and dinner theaters, the figure is 44 percent; for musical groups and artists, 38 percent; and for other performing arts companies, 5 percent.[4]

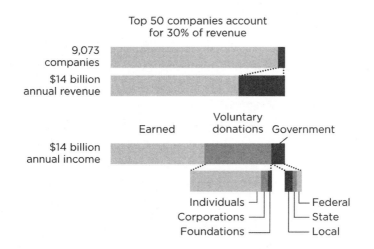

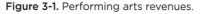

Figure 3-1. Performing arts revenues.

Total private funding to the arts, adjusted for inflation, rose from $9.24 billion in 1999 to $13.67 billion in 2007, fell back during the Great Recession, and has since recovered almost to 2007 levels.[5] These levels of giving have held steady at about 4.5 percent of total philanthropy, which seems rather low until we remember that the bulk of philanthropic donations goes to educational, religious, and health-related organizations.

Government funding of the arts fell during the Great Recession, from about $850 million in 2008 to $700 million as of 2013. The budget of the National Endowment for the Arts was cut during 1995–1996 and has only now recovered to its 1992 level, without adjusting for inflation.

WHO ATTENDS THE PERFORMANCES?

The arts attract small audiences in comparison to major sporting events or rock concerts. The percentages of adults who attended various types of performances at least once during 2008 ranged from 20.8 percent for performing arts festivals to just 9.3 percent for classical music performances, 2.9 percent for ballet, and 2.1 percent for opera (Figure 3-2).

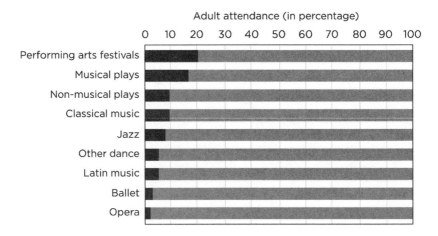

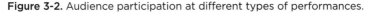

Figure 3-2. Audience participation at different types of performances.

Likewise, classical music radio stations have suffered declining audiences and revenues, which has prompted many stations such as those in New York, Cleveland, and San Francisco to convert to nonprofit status, seeking donations on-air. Yet the Internet has made classical music more accessible than ever.

As is evident to anyone who attends such performances—and as Figure 3-3 shows—audiences are disproportionately white, older, affluent, and highly educated. This should be no surprise if we reflect on the fact that young people acquire an interest in the performing arts, or in any of the fine arts for that matter, primarily from their parents. In this age of slashed education budgets, schools don't play the role they once did in creating a future performing arts audience. (For contrast, consider that two of the authors of this book attended the same public high school in the 1950s in Cleveland, which offered student choruses, a symphony orchestra, symphonic and marching bands, and annual

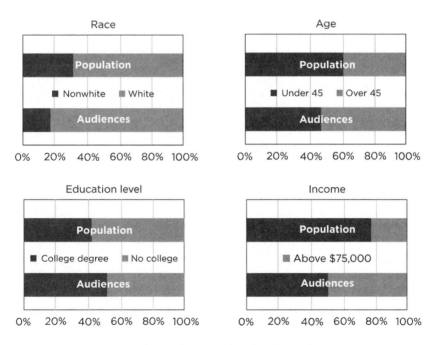

Figure 3-3. Audience demographics for the performing arts.

musical theater productions. Very few public schools are willing to fund such extensive opportunities today.) Children exposed to music and dance in the home are far more likely to become lovers of those art forms, and such families are preponderantly white, well educated, and affluent.

Organizations are well aware of these facts, and most are making concerted efforts to attract younger and more diverse audiences. Symphonies have offered pops concerts for many years and are now experimenting with multimedia productions featuring video projections and collaborations with popular groups. Some have tried 6:30 PM concerts to catch professionals on their way home from work. The New York Philharmonic and the San Francisco Symphony, among others, offer free concerts in park settings. They offer these concerts as a public service, but they must also be thinking about attracting new audiences. (See Chapter 6 to learn what American Ballet Theatre, Carnegie Hall, and the Metropolitan Opera are doing to help solve the problem of dwindling audiences.)

EMPLOYMENT AND COMPENSATION IN THE PERFORMING ARTS

Figure 3-4 shows a breakdown of employment in the arts into four broad categories. Most jobs are found in theater companies, including dinner theaters, and among musical groups. Smaller numbers are found in dance companies and other arts groups. Employment totals in these areas shrank somewhat during the Great Recession and are expected to rebound modestly going forward to 2018.[6]

Hourly compensation is higher in musical groups than in dance or theater. When contemplating hourly wages, we need to remember the capital investments that artists must make. They must amass a great deal of human capital—performing skills—through long years of study and practice. Like most capital assets, human capital depreciates

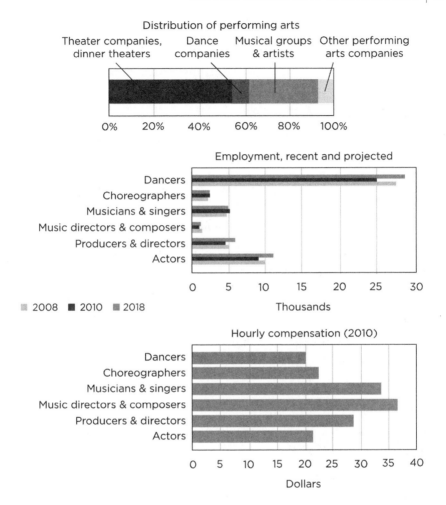

Figure 3-4. Employment and compensation breakdown for the performing arts.

over time. This is a special worry for singers and dancers because (as previously stated) their bodies are their instruments. Instrumental musicians usually have to purchase their own instruments, which can be very expensive: a Stradivarius viola recently fetched $45 million at auction. But instruments generally don't depreciate.

Arts organizations require extensive support staffs. A breakdown by occupation shows that about 41 percent of arts employees actually make the music, compose the music, dance the dances, or choreograph the dances. The other 59 percent take care of makeup, wardrobe, scores, finances, accounting, sales, transportation, security, facilities maintenance, food preparation and service, and a host of other ancillary chores.[7]

Not just in the arts but in the economy generally, labor is becoming more expensive relative to capital. Organizations are under constant pressure to control costs, which very often means reducing head counts. Although recorded music did not eliminate the demand for live musicians as was feared 100 years ago, it has put constant pressure on that demand. Live musical theater still uses live musicians, but far fewer than it once did. A single player is expected to double on clarinet and sax, for example, and there may be only one or two violins. While symphony orchestras have generally retained a full complement of musicians, an orchestra that accompanies a major choral work may be considerably smaller. Ludicrous as it may sound, someone in authority may someday point out the obvious redundancies in symphony orchestras. Why, one might ask, is it necessary to have ten violinists playing one part and ten more playing another? Why not one of each, suitably amplified? Knowing firsthand the magic of live performance, especially when a group gels into a single instrument, we shudder at the thought of such cost-saving measures, but we cannot rule them out.

★ ★ KEYNOTES ★ ★

Questions to Ask Yourself

- Can my arts organization play a greater role in exposing more people in my community to the performing arts? What about parts of my community that aren't traditionally part of the performing arts audience?

- Does knowing the size and salaries of my industry change my desired career path? (Don't answer this question too quickly. We know it can be daunting to realize how small the performing arts industry is, and how low some of the salaries are. This information is included in this chapter to inform you, not to scare you away. Let the information presented here sink in before you rush to conclusions about your career path. Whatever choice you make, you deserve to have all the facts before you make it.)

Tips

- If you're already working for a not-for-profit arts organization, look up your company's financial statements. (See Chapter 5 for more information on financial statements.) You will be able to see whether or not things are going well. If they are, you can let go of any nagging doubts about job security and focus on your work. If they're not going well, you can take action to fix the problem or begin preparations to find work elsewhere.

- People working in other industries, like finance, law, or technology, regularly pay attention to business reporting about their respective professions. Despite the relative smallness of the industry, the performing arts receive a lot of coverage from top media brands like the *New York Times*, the *New Yorker*, and Bloomberg Business. Check in on these major sources of news from time to time or develop the habit of reading them regularly to stay abreast of trends and to see how the public perceives your industry.

Exercises

- Is there an ensemble, company, or institution you dream of working at? Get in touch with somebody there and see if there are any opportunities (and we mean *any*) to get in the door. Anything from an informational interview to an internship making coffee will start a relationship with that organization and give you priceless knowledge about how it works and where you might fit in. It will also put you on the radar of the people who work there. Start with the group's website and see if there is a list of contacts. Especially if you are a student, don't be afraid to email the person in charge and ask for a meeting. Students have a special status in the larger world, and people in every station of life are usually willing to help them out.

• Spend a few moments thinking about the financial, administrative, and managerial side of your career. Imagine yourself balancing the books, making phone calls, sending emails to contacts, or doing other nonartistic activities. What feelings come up? Write down a list of words to describe how you feel. Are the words primarily positive or negative?

—If thinking about the business side of your career fills you with negative emotions like fear and anxiety, don't worry. You're not alone. Many performing artists, even ones with flourishing careers, get nervous about business. But it is important to realize that negative feelings about this necessary part of your work can block you from taking action and being as innovative as you could be. Every job—even that of an artist—has certain aspects that are going to be uncomfortable, seemingly overwhelming, or boring. When you find yourself feeling negative emotions, do your best to let go of them by remembering that you're working in the service of your artistic calling. Instead of fighting against the business side of your career, embrace it and give it the attention and effort it deserves. It won't be half as bad as you think, once you get going. And you'll be amazed at the positive results.

—If thinking about these actions fills you with positive feelings like hope, excitement, and a burst of creative ideas, then you're in good shape. Stay positive about the business side of your career! It can only make your art stronger.

4

THE DIGITAL REVOLUTION AND THE PERFORMING ARTS

Nothing in recent years has had a more profound impact on the performing arts world than the digital revolution. This phrase actually captures two revolutionary changes, one that is benign and one that is very problematic for the performing arts. We think it is worthwhile to review the major changes in recording technology over the last two decades, since one of the intended audiences for this book is recent college and conservatory graduates who did not experience these changes firsthand. We can't tell you what the technological media landscape will look like in the future, but we can at least arm you with knowledge about how it came to look the way it currently does.

The first revolution is the representation of sound by on-off bits rather than analog signals. Vinyl records and magnetic tape are analog media, meaning the intensity of sound is represented by variations in the surface of grooves (records) or variations in magnetic field strength (tape). An analog sound signal is sampled and converted to a pattern of ones and zeros that a laser burns onto a disc. The pattern must be converted back to analog waveforms for sound reproduction.

Compact discs are digital media. The fidelity of digital recordings can be either less or more than that of analog recordings, depending on the sampling rate and the compression ratio. But regardless of fidelity level, digital recordings have no noise like record scratches or tape hiss. Compact discs and disc players require far less physical space to store a given amount of music than LPs or cassette tapes. In turn, solid-state storage formats—flash memory, in particular—have soared in capacity and plummeted in price, rendering compact discs all but obsolete. Thus, an eight-gigabyte thumb drive, sufficient for hundreds of hours of music, is now utterly commonplace. Not long ago, disk drives the size of a washing machine, costing as much as a luxury car, stored about 5 percent of that amount.

The other aspect of the digital revolution is the one we want to focus on, and it is a big problem for the performing arts: the ease with which digital recordings can be copied and distributed. The recording and distribution of sound and moving images no longer requires the distribution and creation of relatively scarce physical objects, and it no longer generates the corresponding value people tend to associate with such objects. What would it take to copy a vinyl LP, for example? You would need expensive, specialized equipment to capture the sound and burn it (in analog form) onto a master disc, which could be used to press copies in vinyl—unthinkable for the average person. In contrast, digital recordings are just a particular kind of computer file encoded according to a particular protocol such as MP3. The high bandwidth (transmission speed) that is available to most of us at very low cost makes it easy to share audio and video files.

At first, greater bandwidth made it possible for users to pass around copies of their music files to their online friends. Young people in particular quickly learned how to "rip" music files from compact discs, and while these files were too large to be sent as email attachments, specialized services soon arose to facilitate sharing. For a time, the leading sharing service was Napster, which appeared in 1999.

To use Napster, you had only to install a piece of software on your personal computer. Users could upload their own music files and download files provided by others. At its peak, there were about 80 million registered Napster users. A great many of them were college students, and many colleges found their campus networks choked with this traffic. Some chose to block Napster and similar services from their campuses not only because of concerns about bandwidth saturation but also because of copyright issues. But individual users seldom felt any qualms about sharing music files, particularly if they had already bought a piece on CD or were searching for a title that was hard to find or perhaps bootlegged. Some simply scoffed at the very idea of having ownership of songs or performances. Their slogan was "Information wants to be free."

The recording industry, represented by the Recording Industry Association of America, was not amused. Neither were some major rock groups who saw their new songs spread around the Internet even before their official release. Several lawsuits were filed, and Napster was shut down in 2001, just two years after its inception.

That same year saw the debut of Apple's iPod and the associated iTunes software. Neither the hardware nor the software was the first of its kind, but as with most of its products, Apple's packaging and promotion were uniquely appealing to consumers. CEO Steve Jobs was successful in designing a system that was at first resisted by recording companies and artists but was eventually accepted. Consumers liked the choice of buying "songs" one at a time for 99 cents rather than having to buy a whole album for $12 or more. ("Song" has become the term that denotes a unit of music, an annoyance to those of us whose tastes run to instrumental music. Beethoven's symphonies do not consist of four "songs" pasted together.)

There is currently a movement away from storage of files on one's own devices to storage in "the cloud." This term refers to storage or computing services provided by large organizations and accessed by customers—both businesses and individuals—via the Internet. The term comes from the fact that users seldom have any idea where their files are physically located; they might as well be off on a cloud somewhere. Cloud services are increasingly attractive to individuals because all the files they create on one of their devices (computer, tablet, smartphone) are immediately available on all their other devices and they need not worry about making backup copies or keeping track of what is current. The cloud trend has induced media consumers to move away from downloading content in favor of streaming it directly over the Internet.

The major music streaming services at this writing are iTunes, Spotify, and Pandora. On iTunes, you are allowed to purchase "songs" for 99 cents (sometimes $1.29); they are then stored on your device and, depending on your settings, in the cloud. Spotify and Pandora are streaming services. For a flat fee (and/or willingness to endure commercial messages), you acquire the right to listen to "songs" that are kept in the cloud, not on your device. To counter this, iTunes introduced a streaming service called iTunes Radio.

These services also make classical music available, and the number of offerings is substantial even though the pop offerings are much larger. A search on Spotify for Shostakovich, for example, turned up a "playlist" of essentially his entire catalog of published works. It behooves young classical musicians to get their work posted on these services. Rubbing shoulders, at least digitally, with the likes of Shostakovich is not a bad prospect at all.

COPYRIGHT LAW AND THE DIGITAL AGE

The digital revolution has raised fundamental questions about the rationale and practice of copyright law and patent law. The U.S. Constitution authorizes exclusive limited-time rights to authors and inventors "to promote the progress of science and useful arts." But there is a downside to the presumed benefits of copyright law. Copyright holders have a monopoly on their work, and if they choose to sell their products, holders of monopolies can generally charge more. It remains an open question as to whether the social benefit from increased production engendered by copyright law outweighs the harm done by monopoly prices.

When you buy a copyrighted book, you are entitled to read it, sell it, give it away, or burn it. But you may not copy it, although you may quote brief passages under the "fair use" doctrine. You may also create parodies. Similar rights and restrictions apply to music and video recordings. But in the past—even after photocopy machines and cassette tape decks appeared—copying was usually more trouble than it was worth. However, now that so much content is in digital form and Internet access is cheap and nearly universal, that is no longer true. The digital revolution has laid bare the real reason why people refrained from making illegal copies of copyrighted works in the past: not so much out of respect for the laws or even for the creators whom the laws protected, but rather because of the sheer impracticality of making such copies. Many of us make copies of copyrighted material from time to time, knowingly or not. When we do it knowingly, we may rationalize our action by telling ourselves that we're not imposing costs on anyone or depriving them of any property because when we copy a file, the original remains in its owner's possession. And the facts show that many copies are being made. An organization called Tru Optik estimates that 10 billion files, including movies, television shows, and games, were downloaded in just the second quarter of 2014. Tru Optik further estimates that 94 percent of these downloads were illegal.[1]

It's important to remember that when we talk about copyright law, we're not talking about something that should regulate your creative life but only the commercial application of it. Take fan fiction, for example. Readers are completely free to reimagine their favorite literary characters in stories of their own making, just as musicians are free to play or modify anybody's music they want. It's the selling of material that draws on the creative work done by others that copyright law is concerned with. It's important to remember that your creative life can and should be boundless. Just be careful about how it intersects with the commercial part of your career.

THE FINANCES OF THE PERFORMING ARTS
IN THE DIGITAL AGE

The profound financial effect of the digital revolution on the recording industry can be seen in Figure 4-1. Since just 2005, total revenues have fallen from about $13 billion per year, of which a small fraction was digital, to under $8 billion in 2013, of which the majority was digital. Total revenues have remained steady since 2010, disregarding inflation.

Not shown in these figures is the proportion of revenues that goes to artists. To be sure, in the old days of sales via physical media, many

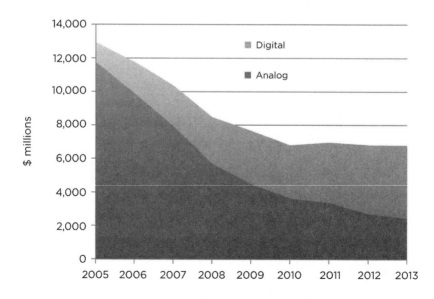

Figure 4-1. The impact of the digital revolution on recording industry revenues.

artists were unhappy with what they saw as the arrogance of recording industry executives and the seemingly arbitrary way in which favored artists were promoted. But at least the chosen artists did get a fairly good cut of revenues. Now, artists often receive a smaller slice of an ever smaller pie. In addition, recording companies are loath to invest in unproven or difficult-to-classify new talent because of the increasingly uncertain prospect that they would ever recoup such investments. Smaller companies may be more willing to try new talent, but they typically lack the resources to promote them vigorously.

A number of popular artists have simply given up on recording revenues as a significant income source. (We have had students who made only a few thousand dollars during a time when their material was downloaded hundreds of thousands of times.) Instead, they have come to view audio and video recordings as promotional material or loss leaders. They hope their recordings will build a following that pays off when they become famous and can attract audiences to live concerts. (And conversely, successful live performances can attract producers.) Groups can put together a music video using cheap recording equipment and readily available editing software. But the odds against them are staggering. While there is no harm in dreaming of fame and fortune, groups should view such projects as fun learning experiences and ways to further their mastery and enjoyment of their chosen art form.

The digital revolution has not spared the world of classical music. Like consumers of popular media, classical music buffs are blessed with an abundance of recordings available at little or no cost. Correspondingly, revenues from recordings have plummeted. A key question going forward is whether classical organizations can succeed with a path like their popular music colleagues are pursuing. Will widespread low-cost availability of recordings spur new interest in concert attendance and philanthropic revenue?

As a case in point, consider the music of the 20th-century Russian composer Dmitri Shostakovich, whom some call the Beethoven of his time. His *Fifth Symphony* is his most popular. The definitive recording of the *Fifth*, many people believe, was made in 1959 by Leonard Bernstein and the New York Philharmonic. (The performance was broadcast live on commercial television, which seems unthinkable in this era of media companies focused on the next quarter's earnings. Praise be to public television for its *Great Performances* series!) We found this recording of the *Fifth* offered on Amazon.com for $13 (CD), $8 (MP3 download), or—surprise!—$13 (cassette) or $13 (vinyl LP). We also found at least a dozen complete performances of the *Fifth* offered free on YouTube, including those led by legendary conductors Leopold Stokowski (1964) and Mstislav Rostropovich (1985) in addition to Bernstein, as well as countless uploads of individual movements. The YouTube offerings are low-fidelity, but that would matter little to a connoisseur intent on comparing interpretations.

CLIMBING TO THE TOP IN THE DIGITAL AGE

Among audiences for popular music, and to a lesser extent in the classical realm, there is a strong feedback effect that results in what Professor Luis Cabral of New York University calls a "winner take all" market.[2] Fans like a particular performer or a particular song largely because their friends like it or they hear it a lot. Popularity begets popularity. Many performers aim to ride this spiral of fame and fortune; few succeed. Those who do succeed get the lion's share, if not literally all the rewards.

This is not a new phenomenon. In the days of Top 40 Radio, starting in about 1955, airplay was the deciding factor in the success of a popular song. As audiences heard a song more often, disk jockeys would play it more, until a point of saturation was reached and it became the next big hit. The process showered handsome rewards on the few artists and producers who made hits this way. Recording companies were keenly aware of the advantages to be gained by getting disk jockeys to play their material (mainly three-minute sides of a 45 RPM disc), in hopes of beginning a spiral of success—so much so that they began to quietly offer payments to DJs to play their records. This practice, a clear conflict of interest, became known as payola. It burst into the open in 1959 and prompted congressional hearings. Alan Freed, the disk jockey who is said to have coined the term "rock and roll," was caught up in the scandal, as was Dick Clark, a prominent television figure of the time whose early career was almost ruined.[3]

Top 40 Radio no longer dominates popular music to the extent it once did. Recording artists no longer care so much about radio air time. Facebook "likes" are the new currency. Likes beget likes in a spiral reminiscent of Top 40 Radio. Because likes are so valuable, many people now offer to generate them for a fee. One way to do this is through advertising. A shadier practice is an echo of payola in which likes can be purchased at websites such as Boostlikes.com. Some of these providers offer likes for as little as a half cent each. This new "industry" generates an estimated $200 million in annual revenue in Facebook likes alone, not counting sidelines such as the manufacturing of Twitter followers, LinkedIn connections, and video views. The work is usually outsourced to offshore "click farms" where workers click away all day for as little as a dollar per thousand clicks.[4]

The foregoing discussion is from the world of popular culture, but the same phenomena can be seen in the classical world, albeit in a more subdued form. Yo-Yo Ma is today's best known cellist; who is second? The Three Tenors were Pavarotti, Domingo, and . . . who? Even in the classical performing arts, it's largely a winner-takes-all game.

★ ★ MARKETING ★ ★

Ralph Waldo Emerson supposedly said, "Build a better mousetrap and the world will beat a path to your door." One of the core messages of this book is that, in this instance, Emerson was dead wrong. To the person who makes the best mousetraps in the world but never bothers to tell anybody, we say, "We hope you have another way of supporting yourself than selling mousetraps." No matter how high the quality of any good or service, it won't be profitable unless people know about it. Without marketing, work can have no commercial value.

Most basically understood, marketing is all the activity that gets a finished product from its place of manufacture into the hands of those who would buy it. It is the process that gets a product to market. Within organizations, marketing is sometimes considered a soft or secondary concern, but without it no business would survive, even those that depend on philanthropic support.

In the performing arts, marketing fills the space between the end of the creative process and the experience of the audience. It's everything that happens from the end of the last rehearsal to the rising of the curtain on opening night.

If you think that the arts are inherently above marketing, just imagine a book without a reader, music without a listener, or a dance performance for nobody. The individual satisfaction of the author or performer matters deeply, but so does the continuance of our great art forms and the joy and sense of meaning that audiences derive from them. Great art deserves as wide an audience as possible. Creating that audience is the mission of the marketing process.

If you're worried that you might not have the temperament for self-promotion, remember that you have a huge advantage over professional advertisers and marketers in the for-profit world. You know your product better and care about it more deeply than they do about their products because your product is yourself. It is the years you've devoted to mastering a difficult skill, one that is essential to the meaning of your life. Don't think of marketing as an insincere prelude to taking people's money. Think of it instead as a way to connect a desire for art with the ability to satisfy that desire. Rather than feeling that your art is somehow cheapened through the marketing process, consider instead that the huge amount of your life that your art has consumed deserves to be honored by as many people as possible.

Core parts of any marketing plan include:

- **Market research.** Who wants your product, and how much might they be willing to pay for it? This includes potential donors as well as paying ticket holders.
- **Branding.** What makes your product different from other, similar products, and how can you convey that in a brief and powerful way? Having a strong brand is the first step to cultivating an audience with a strong relationship to the art you make.
- **Advertising.** How can you project awareness of your product and create a demand for it or tap into existing demand for similar products?
- **Delivery.** What's your plan for the delivery of your product to its consumers? In the case of the performing arts, delivery can take the form of live performance, recordings, streaming Web content, or some as yet unknown combination of all three. Knowing what the finished product will be like can help you create specific demand for it in your audience.

THE SAN FRANCISCO SYMPHONY
IN THE DIGITAL AGE

As we saw in Chapter 3, symphonies and opera companies are fighting for their very existence in the face of declining attendance, aging audiences, and shaky support from foundations and governments. Clearly, these organizations must speak to potential audiences that are younger and more diverse, and they must speak to them in their language. Here is how one organization, the San Francisco Symphony, is doing that.

The Symphony maintains an attractive and functional website at sfsymphony.org. The site offers schedules, online ticket purchases, travel and parking information, and the like. But these sorts of online conveniences are the norm these days—the minimum one would expect. The website also shows that the Symphony is trying hard to reach beyond its traditional audiences, who are disproportionately older, white, and affluent (as discussed in Chapter 3). These potential audiences include the young techies who have become so conspicuous in San Francisco, but also people of Hispanic, African-American, and Asian descent who may never have heard classical music, not even in a recording. A First Timer's Guide page begins at the beginning: "What is classical music?" An answer in the form of a short paragraph is given, as well as a 20-minute video by the Symphony's music director, Michael Tilson Thomas, widely known as MTT. In a TED Talk video,[5] MTT is seated at a piano, casually dressed, and speaking in a conversational tone. He tells how his father influenced his career. He shows how music evokes varying emotions, explaining the very basic concept of major versus minor chords. He illustrates the dramatic transition from despair to joy in the third movement of Beethoven's *Fifth Symphony*. He concludes with a personal story that is worth paraphrasing here.

While visiting a relative in a nursing home, MTT spied a very shaky old man shuffling across the room with a walker. The man sat at a piano and plunked out a few notes while muttering, "boy . . . symphony . . . Beethoven." MTT went to the piano and said, "Friend, by any chance are you trying to play this?" and he began playing a passage from Beethoven's *Violin Concerto*. The old man's eyes widened: "Yes, yes!" he said. "I was a little boy. It was a concerto! Isaac Stern!" MTT marveled that after most of this man's mind had been lost to dementia, the memory of this music remained. "That's why I take every performance so seriously, why it matters so much," says MTT. "I never know who might be there, who might be absorbing it, what will happen to it in their life."

Tilson Thomas is optimistic. "Now I'm excited that there's more possibility than ever in sharing this music," he says, citing the YouTube Symphony Orchestra as one example. Young players from all over the world submitted audition videos online, and those who were chosen were invited to come to New York to assemble as an orchestra and perform in 2009. A repeat event in 2011 was held in Sydney, Australia, and was streamed online to more than 30 million viewers.

A BALLERINA IN THE DIGITAL AGE

Petra Conti is a rising star in the world of ballet. Born in Italy in 1988, she graduated from the National Academy of Dance in Rome at age 18 and thereafter rose quickly through the ranks of Italian ballet. She joined the La Scala Ballet of Milan in 2009 and was promoted to principal dancer in 2011. In 2013, she moved to the Boston Ballet, where she and her husband were, as of 2015, both principal dancers.

Petra belongs to the millennial generation and has grown up in the digital age. This is the generation for whom instant communication, digital media, and social networking are as water to fish. As one would expect, Petra is Internet-savvy and has a website (www.petraconti.it) that provides her biography, photos, videos, and press clippings. There is also a promotional link to a women's fashion designer whose creations she wears in one of her videos. Most of the site is in English, the primary language of the Internet.

Petra's website is not unusual; most featured performers have one. We mention hers as an example that illustrates the opportunities that the Internet provides to performers that would have been unthinkable to 20th-century ballerinas such as the legendary Galina Ulanova (1910–1998). Mme. Ulanova was both a beneficiary and a victim of the Soviet system—a beneficiary in that she gained the attention of Joseph Stalin, who gave her a position at the Bolshoi Ballet, and a victim in that she was not allowed to travel abroad until rather late in her career. Although some of her performances were recorded on film and she may have appeared on Russian television, her opportunities for career advancement were severely limited, not just by the strictures of the Soviet system but by the lack of anything like the communications opportunities that are open to Petra Conti and millennial performers like her. Almost anybody in the world can go online today and learn about Petra Conti, and given a broadband connection, anybody can watch her dance. The Internet will doubtless be the primary vehicle for spreading her fame. Her Web presence may also provide her with further commercial opportunities like the aforementioned link to the fashion designer.

★ ★ KEYNOTES ★ ★

Questions to Ask Yourself

- Are there digital distribution hubs that I can use to disseminate my music or videos of my performances? (These can be blogs, huge commercial sites like iTunes, social media sites, or ways of connecting that are yet to be invented.)
- In an age of easily duplicated and distributed media, is there a new, more important role for live performance? Are there ways I can incorporate this into my business plan?

Tips

- Don't waste time and energy trying to predict the future of digital media technology. Nobody can do that—not even the biggest players in the business. But don't disconnect from changes in the tech landscape. Do your best to keep up and take advantage of the tools your peer group is currently using and paying attention to, but don't waste time being anxious about change.

- Don't spend too much time trying to find the perfect formula for social media success. There is no formula. Musician Laurel Halo gives the best piece of advice we've heard about social media ever: Be yourself. Social media are no different from any other media. They are a way of expressing who you are to people en masse. People won't follow you because of gimmicks. They'll follow you because they love your art and are interested in keeping up with your career. Do be sure to give out plenty of info about where people can get tickets to your next show or buy your next recording, but resist the urge to use your social media platform solely to advertise. That is a surefire turnoff. Give people a window into your life and steady access to your work, and you will keep them interested.

- Just like almost every other aspect of your work, maintaining an online presence will probably work out best if you are open to collaborating with others. You might be able to maintain a Twitter feed on your own, but making a YouTube video, for example, takes a team effort. Tap into your network of friends with needed skills to make the most of your online presence.

- Feedback is a simultaneous disadvantage and advantage to having a Web presence. There is a lot of negative chatter on the Web, and the more you put yourself out there, the likelier it is that some of it will come your way. Try not to take it personally. Take advantage of any positive feedback, and encourage your growing network of supporters. Be sure to take advantage of that rarest type of feedback: constructive criticism. And don't take it personally if you're not getting as much activity back as you're putting into the Web. We've seen tweets and Facebook posts from huge stars generate almost no activity at all, while posts from unknowns go viral overnight. Like so much of your working life, success is sometimes a matter of chance. The important thing to remember is that everybody is expected to have an online presence, so keep plugging away at it.

Exercises

- Pick a few performing artists whose work you admire, and take a look at how they use technology. Look at their Web presence, and try to find out as much as you can about the digital distribution of their work and how that affects their revenue streams. For famous performing artists, this information is likely to be available as news articles on the Web. If you can't find any of this information about less famous performing artists, don't be afraid to contact them directly! If you don't know which performers to pick, start with the ones we profile in Chapter 7. Pay attention as well to how they use the Web to promote themselves and express who they are. Use what you find successful about their work to spark ideas for your own.

READING AND UNDERSTANDING FINANCIAL STATEMENTS

Some people, perhaps artists in particular, think accounting is the most boring subject in the world. You may be one of these people, and you may be tempted to skip this chapter. We hope you won't, though, because a little accounting knowledge can serve you very well. Why? Without modern double-entry bookkeeping, all businesses—including nonprofits—would grind to a halt. Management would be at sea if an organization didn't have accounts to show whether it was on a path toward prosperity or oblivion. You may never be a manager but you should have some understanding of your organization's financial health. The great German poet Johann Wolfgang von Goethe understood this very well. He called double-entry bookkeeping, which we are about to describe, "among the finest inventions of mankind."[1]

Basic accounting—or bookkeeping, if you will—isn't all that difficult. After you complete this chapter, you will know the basic bookkeeping concepts that all businesses, nonprofits, and governments use. To be sure, accounting can get extraordinarily complicated because there are situations where it is very difficult to know how to categorize some items, how to estimate their market value, or whether a particular expense should be carried into the future. That's why some people work very hard to become certified public accountants and why they usually earn big salaries. We won't be concerned with accounting complexities, just the basics.

JUDY'S PERSONAL FINANCES

Here is a simple bookkeeping exercise that will take us lightly through all the categories. It concerns the personal finances of Judy, a hypothetical dancer. Even though individuals and households don't generally do accounting like organizations, it will be instructive for us to do so here.

We start with a snapshot of Judy's assets (what she owns), liabilities (what she owes), and net worth (assets minus liabilities). We track income and expenses over the course of a year, and then take another snapshot at the end of the year. (Incidentally, accounting years, called *fiscal years*, can start on any date, not just January 1.) Let's say Judy's financial situation at the beginning of the year is as follows:

* Assets (what she owns): $45,000
* Liabilities (what she owes): $10,000
* Net worth (assets minus liabilities): $35,000

What do we count as assets? Only things that are durable (they don't wear out too quickly), tangible (you can drop them on your foot), and marketable (they have a dollar value that can at least be estimated). (Note that corporations sometimes list intangible assets, called goodwill. We are not considering this category here.) Judy's most valuable asset is her dancing skill, but because it is well-nigh impossible to attach a dollar figure to this asset, it is intangible and we don't include it in her accounts. To keep simple, we'll ignore assets like a laptop, cell phone, etc., and assume Judy has only the three following assets, whose total value is $45,000:

1. Car: $24,000
2. Dancing apparel: $8,000
3. Checking and savings accounts: $13,000

Why do we include her dancing clothes as an asset but not her street clothes? Because dancing apparel is crucial to her livelihood, as are her car and her bank accounts, while her street clothes are not. We want to emphasize those assets that directly support her professional life.

Judy has just one liability, a car loan whose current balance (principal) stands at $10,000. If she had signed a long-term lease on her apartment, we might count that as a liability, but we'll assume she's renting month-to-month.

During the course of the year, Judy earns $85,000 (which we call her *gross* income) from dancing gigs, teaching, and a little interest on her savings. (As this was written, banks are paying little or no interest. Our point here is that income from bank accounts or investments is a category of income that should be recognized.) She spends $82,000 on living expenses: rent, food, clothing, transportation (mainly her car payment), etc. She has a $3,000 surplus of income over expenses (which we call her *net* income) for the year and she is left in the following position:

- Assets: $42,000
- Liabilities: $8,000
- Net worth: $34,000

You may notice something strange here. Even though she saved $3,000, her net worth fell over the year by $1,000. How can this be? The answer lies in changes in the value of her assets and liabilities.

Depreciation is one such change. This is the loss in value that assets suffer as they wear out. Her car depreciated to $20,000, a loss of $4,000. Although she replaced some dancing apparel, its total value fell to $7,000, a loss of $1,000. On the plus side, Judy added to her assets by increasing her bank balance by $2,000, to $15,000. Finally, she reduced her liabilities by paying down her car loan from $10,000 to $8,000. That leaves her assets and liabilities at:

- Assets: $20,000 + $7,000 + $15,000 = $42,000
- Liabilities: $8,000
- Net worth: $42,000 – $8,000 = $34,000

So we see that even though she enjoyed an earnings surplus, she suffered a slight drop in net worth due mainly to depreciation.

Now let's arrange these numbers in the conventional form that dates back several centuries: the T-account. We show assets in the left-hand column and liabilities and net worth in the right-hand column. Both columns are added, and the sums must always be the same. The books must always balance.

For the beginning of the year we have:

ASSETS		LIABILITIES AND NET WORTH	
Car	$24,000	Car loan	$10,000
Dancing apparel	$8,000		
Checking & saving accounts	$13,000	Net worth	$35,000
Total assets	$45,000	Total liabilities & net worth	$45,000

You can think of net worth as the number that has to be added to liabilities to make the bottom lines match.

We have seen that of Judy's $85,000 income for the year, she spent $82,000 on ordinary living expenses, paid down her car loan by $2,000, and increased her bank balance by $2,000. Her car depreciated by

$4,000 and her dancing apparel by $1,000. These amounts left Judy with the following balance sheet for the end of the year:

ASSETS		LIABILITIES & NET WORTH	
Car	$20,000	Car loan	$8,000
Dancing apparel	$7,000		
Checking & saving accounts	$15,000	Net worth	$34,000
Total assets	$42,000	Total liabilities & net worth	$42,000

Again, we see that even though Judy managed to spend $3,000 less than she took in, her net worth dropped by $1,000 due to $5,000 depreciation offset by a $2,000 bank balance plus a $2,000 car loan reduction.

Now, changing the story a bit, let's say Judy had bought a new car for $32,000, using $5,000 from her savings and a $27,000 car loan (ouch!), while selling her used car for $12,000 and paying off its remaining $8,000 loan balance. (Notice that the $20,000 estimated car value in her balance sheet was way too optimistic since she got only $12,000 for it. Such things happen.) We would record the following income and expense items:

- Income: $12,000 from used car sale
- Expense: pay off $8,000 car loan
- Expense: $5,000 new car down payment

Here's an exercise for you: Construct Judy's balance sheet after completion of this transaction.

THE FINANCES OF A COMMUNITY CHORUS

We now look at the finances of a hypothetical community chorus. Community choruses are a popular outlet for people who love music and have some talent but make their living in other ways. Some choruses are affiliated with colleges or churches, and some are stand-alone. Even with modest expenses, it is all but impossible for a community chorus to get by on ticket sales alone.

A typical chorus needs a conductor, scores, a rehearsal accompanist, a place to rehearse, and a performance venue. While most choristers are volunteers and in fact may be expected to donate money, larger groups sometimes employ ringers, a few paid choristers who may act as section leaders. Conducting a chorus of any size is too much to expect of a volunteer. A conductor who has the requisite background and can devote sufficient time to the job (performing, rehearsing, auditioning, learning scores, courting donors) must be paid. The same is often true of rehearsal accompanists. The larger outfits may need a paid administrator as well. There could also be advertising expenses, hall rental fees, and travel expenses.

Expenses may not end there. Suppose, for example, a group is ambitious enough to stage Carl Orff's *Carmina Burana*, a popular and very demanding piece. Like all major choral works, *Carmina* includes prominent solo parts. Sometimes a chorister is good enough to step into a solo role, but the solo parts in *Carmina* are quite challenging and in fact call for that rare bird, a countertenor. Paid soloists are very desirable for this piece, although advanced voice students can sometimes be had for little or no compensation.

To do the piece justice, the chorus must employ a full orchestra. For some works, a piano transcription makes an acceptable substitute for an orchestra, but not for *Carmina Burana*, whose movements run the gamut from subtle lyricism to blasting horns. Again, amateurs may be available, but at least the key parts like the concertmaster or the oboe or horn players should be professionals. Sometimes the Musicians' Union will cooperate and waive the usual union pay scale.

A typical community chorus would have very little in the way of assets or liabilities. It might be allowed free use of rehearsal and performance spaces or it might rent them, but it would not own them. It might own a piano and perhaps a collection of scores, though choristers are often asked to buy their own scores. The chorus's principal asset would probably be a bank balance. It might have borrowed money and might have deferred expenses, but otherwise there would be very little to count as liabilities.

Thus, the finances of a community chorus would pretty much be a matter of cash flow. It would have to keep enough cash on hand to allow for uncertain ticket receipts in addition to recurring expenses. Fundraising would have to be a top priority. While smaller groups may resort to bake sales and such, a larger group would be wise to cultivate a permanent sponsor. For example, a local bank or the local electric utility might see sponsorship as a way to burnish its image with the local populace. The company's logo could be featured prominently on the chorus's printed materials and website.

Here is the year-end balance sheet of our make-believe chorus.

COMMUNITY CHORUS BALANCE SHEET, YEAR-END 2015			
ASSETS, DEPRECIATED		LIABILITIES	
Piano	$2,200	Unpaid bills	$225
Scores	$1,500	Loan from patron	$9,500
Office equipment	$400	Total liabilities	$9,725
Bank account	$4,200	Net worth	-$1,425
Total assets	$8,300	Liabilities plus net worth	$8,300

Notice that the chorus has a negative net worth and is technically insolvent. The patron who made the loan is probably worried but not inclined to press the chorus into bankruptcy.

We now look at income and expenses for our chorus, summed over the year 2015.

COMMUNITY CHORUS INCOME AND EXPENSES, 2015			
INCOME		EXPENSES	
Ticket sales	$16,212	Salaries and benefits	$12,011
Gift shop net income	$413	Orchestra	$8,012
Food and beverage net income	$823	Soloists	$8,900
Silent auction net income	$4,213	Advertising	$250
Other donations	$9,412	Equipment rental	$750
		Interest payment	$450
Total income	$31,073	Total expenses	$30,373
		Surplus	$700

The chorus earned a small surplus (profit) of $700 for the year.

TWO KINDS OF FINANCIAL DISTRESS

There are two basic ways an organization can get in financial trouble, be it a for-profit company, a nonprofit, a government, or a household. The less serious problem is called *illiquidity*, a situation where there is not enough cash to pay bills coming due. Assuming the organization has sufficient noncash assets, this problem can usually be remedied by borrowing against those assets, by selling some of them, or by quickly generating more income. A onetime liquidity crunch may not be very serious, but a series of such crunches can lead to the more serious problem of *insolvency*. This occurs when an organization's liabilities exceed its assets. At this stage, management's options are limited. Creditors (those to whom the organization owes money) may force the organization into bankruptcy, which may be followed by restructuring of its obligations or liquidation—in other words, termination of the organization. Of course, management can appeal to creditors to refrain from pushing for bankruptcy and to patrons for emergency donations. If you find yourself under serious pressure from creditors and truly unable to pay the bills without going under, know that the status of your organization as a not-for-profit and an arts organization can help you survive. While we're not at all advocating taking advantage of anybody's good faith, it's okay to remind your creditors that you're not in business to make a profit but to contribute to your community, and you can ask for leniency.

Because liquidity (availability of cash to meet current obligations) is important, any organization, whether for-profit or not, must keep a close eye on *cash flow*. As the term implies, this category tracks the cash coming in minus the cash going out during some time period such as a quarter or a fiscal year. Cash flow is not the same as profit, which is earnings minus expenses. One difference is that some kinds of incoming cash do not count as earnings. Examples are proceeds from sales of assets, money borrowed from a bank, or proceeds of sales of securities (shares of stock or bonds). Likewise, some kinds of outgoing cash do not count as expenses. Examples include purchases of durable equipment that is depreciated over time, payment of interest to bondholders, or payment of dividends to shareholders.

Notwithstanding her reduced net worth at year end, Judy's cash situation is solid. She enjoyed a $3,000 positive cash flow during the year and ended up with $15,000 in the bank. She would be able to weather a short-term slowdown in her income with little difficulty.

As the community chorus example shows, nonprofit organizations can and do earn profits, although "surplus" is the more common term. While profits are not their primary mission, competent managers of nonprofits keep an eye on the bottom line so as to avoid excessive or extended losses. If you are considering joining an arts organization, you should pay attention to its finances. You want some assurance that the group will remain in business for the near future, at least. Has it been losing money? How has it made up losses?

FINANCIAL REPORTS

All publicly held for-profit corporations are required to issue reports of their financial situation. They publish quarterly and annual reports and file various forms with the Securities and Exchange Commission, which are available to anyone. Their tax returns, however, are generally not made public.

Nonprofit reporting requirements are a little different. Excepting religious institutions, most nonprofits must file Internal Revenue Service Form 990, which is supposed to justify continuation of their tax-exempt status. These forms can be found on websites like www.guidestar.org.

THE PROSPERITY OF THE
SAN FRANCISCO SYMPHONY

We retrieved Form 990 for the year 2011 for the San Francisco Symphony. It is 53 pages long, although many pages are blank because they are not applicable to the Symphony. The very first entry shows the Symphony's mission statement: "Enriches, serves, and shapes cultural life throughout the spectrum of Bay Area communities."

Performers and audiences alike naturally prefer to focus on the music, not finances. But as we stress throughout this book, both performers and audiences need to pay some attention to financial matters. Over the last 40 years, the San Francisco Symphony has advanced greatly on several fronts. The quality of the performers and the music has improved, the Symphony moved to a hall of its own, its reputation has spread, and although there have been rough patches, including a couple of musicians' strikes, its finances have generally been stable.

Figure 5-1 shows the Symphony's balance sheet for 2011, taken from its Form 990. The first thing to note for any balance sheet is how the numbers are expressed. The Symphony's numbers are expressed in

		BEGINNING OF YEAR 2011	END OF YEAR 2011
1	Cash, noninterest bearing	$1,241,002	$716,084
3	Pledges and grants receivable, net	$26,433,053	$21,213,894
4	Accounts receivable, net	$2,756,228	$2,491,584
7	Notes and loans receivable	$1,966,757	$2,270,803
8	Inventories for sale or use	$755,433	$662,696
9	Prepaid expenses and deferred charges	$9,700,083	$5,968,878
10	Land, buildings, and equipment less accumulated depreciation	$17,995,867	$18,064,226
11	Investments—publicly traded securities	$181,535,455	$186,859,223
12	Investments—other securities	$53,990,047	$52,488,428
14	Intangible assets		
15	Other assets	$10,385,657	$9,485,905
16	Total assets	$306,759,580	$300,320,701
17	Accounts payable and accrued expenses	$4,532,218	$5,081,062
19	Deferred revenue	$13,158,974	$12,259,056
25	Other liabilities	$28,383,873	$39,050,516
26	Total liabilities	$44,075,065	$56,390,634
27	Unrestricted net assets	$62,108,800	$43,213,422
28	Temporarily restricted net assets	$67,823,806	$65,507,368
29	Permanently restricted net assets	$132,752,109	$135,209,277
33	Total net assets or fund balances	$262,684,515	$243,930,067
34	Total liabilities and net assets/fund balances	$306,759,580	$300,320,701

Note: Based on Form 990 filed by the San Francisco Symphony for 2011. Blank lines have been omitted.

Figure 5-1. A San Francisco Symphony balance sheet.

whole dollars, but large corporations sometimes present numbers in thousands or even millions of dollars so as to reduce clutter.

Line 1 shows $1.2 million cash on hand. Since the Symphony spends about $78 million per year (as shown in Figure 5-3 on page 76), that was enough cash to pay only about 1.5 weeks' worth of expenses. However, a balance sheet is a snapshot, and it's possible this figure was a lot higher at other times during 2011. If it got much lower, the Symphony could have a liquidity problem, i.e., a cash crunch.

Line 3 indicates donor pledges that have been made but have not yet been paid. Some of these promises may not be kept. If this was a bank, we would see allowances for doubtful loan repayments, but non-profits usually do not attempt to make any such estimates with regard to pledges.

When an organization pays a bill like an insurance premium that covers the year ahead, it is called a prepaid expense. The payment has been made but most of the benefit (the insurance coverage) still lies ahead. The excess is counted as an asset and marked down as the year goes by. Unpaid bills are the opposite; they would be subtracted from any prepaid expense (see Line 9).

The city of San Francisco owns Davies Symphony Hall, where the Symphony performs, so its value is not an asset of the Symphony. The Symphony does own many kinds of equipment, which are depreciating assets. Also, the Symphony has paid for improvements to Davies Hall that are counted as assets; they are depreciated as the time approaches when they may need to be redone. The amount shown on Line 10 is the result of subtracting about $16 million worth of depreciation from original costs of about $34 million for those assets.

Depreciation can be a tricky business. Accountants assign useful lives to assets and then write them down (reduce their stated value) every year. An ordinary desk may be assigned a ten-year life, yet it remains perfectly serviceable for decades, but the accounting rules say it has no value once it reaches age ten. In contrast, a laptop computer may be assigned a three-year life, but after just two years—at which time its stated value is one-third of its purchase price—it may be discarded in favor of a tablet. Income is generated when an asset is sold for more than the depreciated value on its balance. Expense is incurred if it is sold for less—as when Judy sold her car for $12,000 even though its estimated value had been $20,000.

Most nonprofits of medium or large size have an endowment—a portfolio of income-producing assets. Donors can generally specify whether their contributions are to be used for immediate expenses or are to be added to the endowment. Harvard University has a whopping $32 billion endowment that is managed by a highly compensated professional team. The endowment income provides major support to the university's operations. Organizations generally spend only the income from their endowments, not the principal. However, they sometimes "invade" their endowments, spending some of the principal. They may say they are borrowing from their endowment, but whether they do or not, invasion of endowment principal generally suggests desperation.

The San Francisco Symphony has an endowment, most of which is invested in publicly traded securities (probably stocks and bonds, Line 11) and other securities that are not detailed (Line 12). Endowment income amounted to about $4.0 million in 2011, up from $3.2 million during the previous year but still down from the prerecession high of $5.3 million. This income is not a huge contributor to the Symphony's annual income, but it can make a big difference at the margin of a good year or a bad year.

As we saw with Judy's balance sheet, total assets (Line 16) must exactly equal the sum of total liabilities (Line 26) plus total net assets (Line 33), and they do (Line 34).

Figure 5-2 shows revenues earned in 2011. Right away, we see that contributions (Lines 1) amounted to more than half the Symphony's revenue for 2011. In other words, ticket sales cover only about half of expenses, and this fact is made clear to subscribers, who are strongly urged to add a donation to the price of their tickets. Line 8 shows that fundraising expenses were a lot larger than the amount raised. There is probably an explanation for this—perhaps those expenses generated

	CONTRIBUTIONS, GIFTS, GRANTS		
1c	Fundraising campaigns	$7,804,238	
1e	Government grants	$776,100	
1f	All other contributions	$21,143,801	
		Total	$29,143,801
	PROGRAM SERVICE REVENUE		
2a	Concert & related revenue	$25,967,992	
2b	Volunteer Council	$179,691	
2c	SFS Media	$82,161	
		Total	$26,230,844
	OTHER REVENUE		
6d	Rental income	$28,463	
7a	Asset sales, gross amount	$40,512,591	
7b	Less cost of sales	-$40,599,437	
7c	Gain (loss)	-$86,846	
8a	Fundraising revenue, excluding line 1c	$1,699,601	
8b	Less direct expenses	-$6,476,741	
8c	Net income (loss) from fundraising	-$4,777,140	
10a	Gross sales of inventory	$1,474,014	
10b	Less cost of goods sold	-$996,978	
10c	Net income (loss) from sales of inventory	$477,036	
11a	Food & beverage from patrons, net	$337,648	
11b	Miscellaneous	$94,600	
		Total revenue	**$56,118,312**

Figure 5-2. A San Francisco Symphony statement of income.

some funds that will be part of the income for future years. (If you were interviewing for a job with the Symphony, you might ask your interviewer about this. Although there is a risk that such a question might be viewed as impertinent, it would show that you have made some effort to understand the Symphony's finances. Interviewers like job applicants to show they have done some homework.)

The Symphony's management personnel are paid well. Although not shown in Figure 5-3 (expenses), elsewhere in Form 990 we find that Executive Director Brent Assink received $638,857 in total compensation during 2011, and Concertmaster Alexander Barantschik got $560,010. For some reason, the salary of music director Michael Tilson Thomas is not listed on Form 990, though a newspaper report put his pay at $1.6 million for 2008.[2]

Most businesses of medium to large size, and some small ones, offer employee retirement benefits as well as health insurance and other "perks." There are two basic categories of retirement plans: (1) pensions, also called defined-benefit plans, and (2) defined-contribution plans, mainly 401(k) plans for businesses or the equivalent 403(b) for nonprofits. Pension plans provide retired employees with a certain monthly income for the rest of their lives, the amount of which is based on their salary and years of service. This is a risky proposition for the company because of uncertainty about when people will retire, how long they will live, and whether the assets in the pension plan will throw off sufficient income to cover obligations. Many government bodies and some corporations are in trouble because of under-funded pension liabilities. Except in special circumstances, organizations with pension plans must contribute something to their pension plans to keep them financially sound. The Symphony's contribution for 2011 appears on Line 8 of Figure 5-3.

Pension plans are becoming less common in the business world because of the uncertainties just mentioned. Many companies have switched to defined-benefit plans in which the employer and employee each contribute to a fund that is invested, usually in stocks and bonds or mutual funds. Employees generally have some say as to which investments they want in their account. Upon retirement, an employee receives a lump sum, at which time the employer's involvement ceases. The retiree decides whether and how to spend his retirement money, in accordance with tax laws. Most pension plans are

1	Grants to governments and organizations in the U.S.	$79,217
5	Compensation of officers, directors, trustees, and key employees	$1,749,082
7	Other salaries and wages	$28,790,241
8	Pension plan contributions	$4,929,197
9	Other employee benefits	$5,076,859
10	Payroll taxes	$1,993,556
11	Fees for service	
11a	Legal	$9,902
11c	Accounting	$178,347
11d	Lobbying	$12,251
11e	Professional fundraising	$459,189
11f	Investment management	$139,577
11g	Other nonemployee fees	$364,661
12	Advertising and promotion	$1,680,714
13	Office expenses	$1,392,527
14	Information technology	$296,222
16	Occupancy	$558,779
17	Travel	$91,342
22	Depreciation, depletion, amortization	$1,128,007
23	Insurance	$417,708
24	Other expenses	
24a	Concert production	$19,157,269
24b	Amortization	$3,466,497
24c	Consulting fees	$2,506,670
24d	Plant fund—other	$1,480,200
24f	Other expenses	$2,379,012
	Total functional expenses	$78,338,012

Figure 5-3. A San Francisco Symphony statement of expenses.

found in unionized organizations such as the Symphony or in government agencies.

If you work for any kind of organization that offers retirement benefits, you should take full advantage of them if at all possible. This is especially true if your employer offers to match all or part of the contributions that you have taken from your salary, because matching funds are free money, pure and simple. With or without matching, the compounded value of retirement savings begun at an early age can be enormous when retirement comes.

THE DEMISE OF THE SAN JOSE REPERTORY THEATRE

The financial statements of the San Francisco Symphony present a picture of an organization in pretty good financial health. The San Jose Repertory Theatre was a very different story. After years of deficits and a bailout from the San Jose city government, the Rep closed its doors in 2014 and filed for Chapter 7 bankruptcy.

This was an organization about a tenth the size of the Symphony. It had several advantages going for it: a talented group of resident actors and directors, live presentations, most of them produced by the Rep itself, and its own 584-seat theater located in the heart of downtown San Jose, California, a short distance from a major state university. San Jose is a city with a population of 1 million (6 million in the entire Bay Area), including abundant Silicon Valley wealth and talent. The city government was a major supporter, seeing the Rep as the centerpiece of its efforts to develop downtown San Jose as a cultural and entertainment attraction. Following the Rep's demise, there was quite a bit of speculation about the causes of its failure. Many noted that the San Jose Symphony had been swept away by the dot-com bust of 2001, even given a talented conductor and a new Performing Arts Center. This suggests that San Jose, tech wealth notwithstanding, still lacks the critical mass of support needed to establish major cultural institutions. No doubt this is partly due to the magnetic pull of San Francisco, 50 miles north.

The Rep's summary financials are shown in Figure 5-4. The income statement shows that ticket sales covered a little over half of expenses, which is fairly typical. Rental of its hall to outsiders actually

INCOME FOR 2011			
Contributions, gifts, grants		$1,966,648	
Program service revenue		$2,436,469	
Investment income		$17,368	
Royalties		$1,730	
Rental income, gross	$46,538		
Rental expenses	$49,032		
Net rental income (loss)		-$2,494	
Fundraising events, gross	$145,687		
Fundraising expense	$46,903		
Net fundraising		$98,784	
Inventory sales, gross	$18,884		
Cost of goods sold	$18,852		
Net income from sales		$32	
Total revenue		**$4,518,537**	
EXPENSES FOR 2011			
Compensation of officers	$120,265		
Other salaries and wages	$2,100,279		
Payroll taxes	$273,891		
Other	$2,327,089		
Total expenses	**$4,821,524**		
ASSETS AT YEAR-END 2011	**LIABILITIES**		
	Secured mortgages and notes	$791,499	
	Unsecured notes and loans	$2,015,225	
	Other	$2,069,043	
	Total liabilities		$4,875,767
	Net worth		($109,207)
Total	**$4,766,560**	**Liabilities and net worth**	**$4,766,560**

Figure 5-4. San Jose Repertory Theatre financials for 2011.

resulted in a loss. One out of every three dollars received in fundraising events went to fundraising expenses, which is high. Sales of assets resulted in a gain of just $32, but that figure may be deceiving. As we have said, valuation of assets is tricky, and it may be that the items sold were no longer of any use to the Rep even though they had been assigned a value of $18,852. Repeating the pattern of previous years, the Rep sustained an operating loss of about $300,000 for the year. This left the company in a position of negative net worth: insolvency.

We have said that insolvency is a very serious matter, but we should qualify that a bit. For one thing, the accuracy of an insolvency verdict depends on whether assets are realistically valued. If it turns out that assets have been overvalued—as Judy's car was prior to its sale—an organization's net worth may turn negative, rendering it at least technically insolvent; of course, undervaluation of assets can have the opposite effect. An organization's track record and future prospects are also important. If there is reason to believe that an insolvent organization's financial embarrassment is temporary and that a turnaround is likely, creditors (those to whom money is owed, such as suppliers, bondholders, or employees) may decide to be patient. Otherwise, things can go wrong in a hurry. Bondholders may press for repayment and perhaps file involuntary bankruptcy proceedings—a last resort given hefty legal costs. Supporters may decide further donations would be wasted. Employees may refuse to take cuts in pay and benefits. All of these can trigger a death spiral. Such was the sad fate of the San Jose Repertory Theatre: The doors closed in 2014 as the Rep filed for bankruptcy. At this writing, it is not known what the city of San Jose will do with the empty theater. The city's financial difficulties (particularly its pension liabilities) make it unlikely that anything new will open there soon.

★ ★ HOW TO WRITE A BUSINESS PLAN ★ ★

Professionals in almost any field sooner or later find it necessary to write a proposal or business plan. Business schools teach this subject in depth, and we can only review it very briefly.

The most important key to writing a successful proposal, whether it is a grant proposal or a commercial business plan, is to put yourself in your readers' shoes. Among other things, try to:

- **Understand your readers' business so you can show them how you will help them fulfill their mission.** Without saying so directly, lead your readers to believe that your work can make them look good to their boss or clients.
- **Be respectful of their time.** Don't send a proposal that does not fall within (or close to) the mission of your target organization. Write succinctly and directly, avoiding unnecessary jargon.
- **Where there are risks or uncertainties, do not try to hide them.** Be candid and indicate as best you can how you propose to address these problems.
- **Put your best foot forward.** However, do not exaggerate and do not feign qualifications that you don't really have.

While there are no strict rules as to how a proposal should be organized, the following topics can be considered core elements:

- **The needs that drive your proposal and the benefits you believe will accrue from your work.**
- **The strategies you have in mind and how you will implement them.**
- **The basic purpose of your proposal.** Even if you're responding to a request for a proposal, where the readers know perfectly well

what the purpose is, repeat it anyway to show you're on the right track. State very briefly what you intend to accomplish and how.

- **The key individuals who will be involved in the work.** Describe how their experience and education qualify them for the job.
- **Financial and budget information.** Do not underestimate the start-up capital you will need. Allow for contingencies; expect unexpected expenses! You will find it harder to return to the well, should you run out of money, than to get enough at the beginning.

IN SUMMARY

We already said that for-profit organizations and nonprofits are very much alike in many respects. You probably wouldn't know just from looking at the expenses in Figure 5-3 whether this entity was a for-profit or a nonprofit. On top of wages and salaries, you see benefits, payroll taxes (nonprofits must usually pay Social Security tax and disability tax), and contributions to the pension plan. The organization incurs the usual professional expenses as seen on Line 11: legal, accounting, investment management, etc. Investment management fees are, as one would hope, a fraction of 1 percent of assets. The organization advertises, pays an office staff, and uses computers (Lines 12, 13, and 14). It even shows a small lobbying expense (Line 11d), and it made donations to other nonprofits (Line 1). All of these expenses are typical of for-profit companies as well as nonprofits. A for-profit business, unlike a nonprofit, would also show income tax payments and possibly dividend payments to shareholders.

★ ★ KEYNOTES ★ ★

Questions to Ask Yourself
- Do I know the financial health of the organizations where I am seeking work? (Getting a sense of the financial health of an organi-

zation where you are interviewing for a job is great for two reasons. First, it can help you determine if you're likely to have a job in the future, and second, it can arm you with a great deal of knowledge that you can deploy in your job interview, if it seems appropriate. Knowing about the finances of the place you are interviewing sends a strong signal that you are thorough and care enough about the organization to learn more about it on your own time.)

- Do I have a sense of my own financial health? Do I know which questions to ask to determine it? Am I afraid to ask these questions? (In writing this chapter, we're not implying that you need the financial literacy of an accountant to be responsible about money, either your own or that of your organization. But we are saying that knowing how to ask and answer basic questions about money is an essential life skill.)

Tips

- Any not-for-profit organization (most performing arts organizations fall into this category) has to file regular reports of its financial situation with the government. The reporting requirements for nonprofits are greater than they are for for-profits. These reports, as well as other valuable information, are available online at the websites of GuideStar, Charity Navigator, and the Foundation Center, among other organizations. When looking over financial reporting data, you will find a lot of terminology and forms of notation that may seem overwhelming or unfamiliar at first, but you'd be surprised how much of the information is relatively easy to understand if you stick with it even for just a few minutes. You will be able to find the mission statement of the organization in question, salaries of the highest paid employees, how much money the organization made in any given year, and footnotes explaining anything extraordinary, both good and bad, about the group's financial situation.

- Try to embrace the fun side of doing the numbers. Numbers can be like a puzzle that you get to figure out or a new language to learn that will get you further in the world. Don't think of your finances as separate from your artistic dreams. Think of them as the building blocks of your dream.

- If you are a student, look to see if there are any classes in entrepreneurship or business at your school. If there are no official business classes, go to your career services office or guidance counselor and ask if there are any resources you can tap into to start developing the business side of your career. If those resources aren't available, find somebody on the faculty of your school or in your community whom you trust, and ask her about practical ways to develop your career. It's never too late to get help, and it is always closer at hand than you think.

Exercises

- Calculate your net worth the way we do for Judy in this chapter. Don't worry about including an accounting of everything you own. Just start with the major items and see what you come up with. Try out this exercise periodically to see whether your net worth increases or decreases.

- Take the table we provide for the finances of the community chorus in this chapter and try to fill in your own numbers (estimates are fine) for an existing arts organization. This is your first step toward knowing how to balance the books.

- Follow the money. Pick an arts organization and find out how it is funded. It can be a major organization like the Metropolitan Opera or the San Francisco Symphony, or it can be a smaller organization, maybe one in your community. To get the most from this exercise, pick an organization that performs the kind of work you want to do or that's the size of what you hope to create. Examine at least two years of the organization's financial statements and see how much money is coming in, from where, and how it is spent. What are the organization's assets? What are its biggest expenses? Be sure to read any footnotes in the financial statements, as that is often where some of the most crucial and fascinating information is located. As we've said, it can be powerful to investigate an organization you're hoping to work for. Examining its financials can give you a sense of the organization's long-term prospects and what the salary ranges of its top officers are, or at the very least give you some insightful questions to ask during an interview.

- Try your hand at creating a business plan! First, brainstorm potential ideas, without worrying too much about how crazy or unworkable they might sound. Then, take the one that excites you most and submit it to the planning process we talk about in this chapter. Dream big, but don't underestimate how much time, effort, and cash you'll need to get started.

- Have an entrepreneurial workshop. Gather some friends and colleagues and put your heads together to discuss existing ideas and brainstorm new ones for performing arts projects. The group doesn't have to be made up of just performing artists. In fact, the more diverse the gathering, the richer and more creative the discussion is likely to be. Take some time to prepare a presentation about your idea. Give everybody a chance to give their feedback or to riff on your project and come up with productive variations. Make an effort to create an atmosphere where the focus is on brainstorming and constructive criticism. Don't worry about your idea being perfect, and don't let the discussion get too critical. Especially in the beginning, new and potentially successful projects are going to be rough, imperfect, and not entirely thought out. This is entirely natural. Bring the same tolerance for the creative process to your entrepreneurial workshop that you would to a collaborative work of theater, dance, or music that is still in process.

ESSENTIAL LESSONS FROM THE GREAT MANAGERS

In this chapter, we present profiles of four visionary administrative leaders of top New York performing arts organizations:

1. Peter Gelb, general manager of the Metropolitan Opera
2. Sir Clive Gillinson, executive and artistic director of Carnegie Hall
3. Meredith "Max" Hodges, former executive director of Gallim Dance (now executive director of the Boston Ballet)
4. Rachel S. Moore, former CEO of American Ballet Theatre (now president and chief executive of the Music Center in Los Angeles)

While there are no standard career paths to follow in the performing arts, even on the management side of things, there are lessons to be learned from every success story. In this chapter, we offer insights and advice from the careers of these four dynamic leaders.

The material here is drawn from original research, from one-on-one interviews, and from the presentations Gelb, Gillinson, Hodges, and Moore personally gave to the students of "Understanding the Profession: The Performing Arts in the 21st Century." By reading this chapter, you will be getting a front-row seat in the class. You will also be getting a behind-the-scenes look at how the performing arts business functions at the highest level.

PETER GELB, GENERAL MANAGER, THE METROPOLITAN OPERA

AUTHENTICITY

When answering questions, Peter Gelb speaks out of one side of a smile and fixes the person he is addressing with a pair of intense, twinkling eyes. He deploys an even tone that is the same no matter whom he is talking to. Whether it is a nervous diva about to go onstage, an audience of millions watching one of his *Live in HD* broadcasts, or a Juilliard or Fordham University senior, you get the same Peter Gelb. As he tells it, it was just this authenticity that got him the job he currently holds and that has guided him throughout his career.

Gelb's title is general manager, which means he wields chief executive and artistic authority at the Metropolitan Opera, the world's largest not-for-profit performing arts organization. The Met has 1,600 year-round employees and can employ up to 1,600 more during its performance season.[1] It has an annual budget of more than $300 million, which dwarfs the budgets of all other performing arts companies in the United States and most cultural organizations of any kind.[2] The Met occupies center stage in the global opera world. Fans, singers, and other opera companies from every country look to the Met as the most prominent opera venue on earth.

Gelb has been general manager since 2006, and it is difficult to imagine that he was once an unlikely choice for the job. Gelb's predecessor, Joseph Volpe, started out as an apprentice carpenter at the Met and worked his way up through the ranks. Conversely, Gelb jumped over to the Met from his post as a transformational—some would say controversial—head of Sony Classical, where he had broken the taboo against recording movie soundtracks (*Titanic*; *Crouching Tiger, Hidden Dragon*), which before his tenure were considered too lowbrow to be recorded and marketed to classical movie audiences. He also started the commissioning of original contemporary classical works for release on the label. Before Sony, Gelb had worked as an agent for Columbia Artists Management. He later started and headed up the Sony subsidiary CAMI Video, producing classical music telecasts and documentaries, some for the Met itself, many of which won him Emmys. But his only jobs in opera proper had been as a Met usher at the age of 16 and a stint as freelance head of the Met's media department in the late 1980s.

All of this gave him a reputation as a showman and popularizer rather than a potential guardian of opera as high art. His appointment to the Met's top job raised the hackles of some traditional opera fans, while galvanizing those who believed that without engaging changing tastes, opera was doomed to extinction. There was controversy about his appointment not only before his first day on the job but even before his job interview.

"I was literally the last person they spoke to," said Gelb, talking to the students of "Understanding the Profession: The Performing Arts in the 21st Century."[3] "When I became general manager in 2006, the Met was already imperiled. That was obvious, or else they probably wouldn't have hired me." Even before the effects of the 2008 global financial meltdown, the Met's finances had been suffering. Midway through the three seasons before he took over, the opera house had been forced to cut its budget. Gelb is quick to point out that he is a great opera lover, but that during his job interview he didn't harbor any illusions about the art form's declining fortunes.

Before Gelb's job interview, average seasonal attendance at opera houses across the United States had been in decline, dropping from 42,000 tickets sold on average per house in 2002 to 39,000 in 2006.[4] As a percentage of full capacity, ticket sales at the Met itself had dropped from around 90 percent in 1980 to only 79 percent in 2005, the year Gelb signed his contract with the Met.[5] During his interview, Gelb spoke to the search committee about what he would later famously call "a cultural and social rejection of opera as an art form."[6] His fears proved prophetic. Here is just a partial list of American opera companies that have closed since 2008: Opera Pacific (Orange County, California), Connecticut Opera, Spokane Opera, Cleveland Opera, Baltimore Opera,[7] Orlando Opera,[8] Opera Boston,[9] and—most notoriously—New York City Opera,[10] which shut down in October 2013 after 70 years in existence (see Chapter 2).

It was an acute awareness of the high stakes for opera's survival that led Gelb to be so candid with the Met's search committee, which included Beverly Sills (one of the greatest opera singers in history, spoken of in the same breath with Maria Callas and Enrico Caruso). Sills was chair of the Met's board of directors and had reached out to Gelb, inviting him to interview for the top job.

During his interview, Gelb looked straight at the members of the search committee and told them that their beloved opera house was fast losing relevance. He compared the Met to an island settlement that had lost touch with the mainland. If he were hired, said Gelb, he would be fearless about making big changes at the institution that would link it back up to the larger landmass of American culture.

Gelb's candor—including telling one of the world's great opera singers that the art form she had devoted her life to was headed for near extinction—could easily have put him out of the running for the most coveted offstage job in opera. Instead, it bumped him to the top of the list. It was Sills herself whose support proved decisive. A word in Gelb's favor from her mattered not only to the other members of the board but eventually to the galaxy of New York society, in which the Metropolitan Opera is a brightly burning star, and from which the Opera draws its major financial support. Gelb was called back and offered the job the next day, and just one day after that, he signed a contract.[11]

Gelb's authenticity helped him not only get his job but carry it out, too. Sills's initial support started Gelb's relationship to the Met's board off on the right foot. Sills stepped down from the board in 2005 and passed away in 2007, but Gelb and his innovations (detailed below) have continued to enjoy direct and enthusiastic support from the board and many of its key donors. First impressions do indeed matter a great deal, and it's important to be authentic and fearless when you make them.

THE TECHNOLOGY GAMBLE

Gelb's most prominent achievement has been to harness technology to bring the Met's workings, both onstage and off, before the eyes of millions of people outside the opera house. He created the Met's *Live in HD* broadcasts, which transmit real-time, high-definition video of select performances each year to movie theaters around the world.

The Met has a long tradition of using live broadcast media. Its radio broadcasts helped an entire generation, among them Gelb, to learn about and appreciate opera. During his class presentation at Juilliard, Gelb displayed an old black-and-white photo of a gymnasium floor packed with rapt adults and children. They were gathered to listen not to a sports broadcast, as the image might imply, but to a live opera on the radio. It was not uncommon for groups to gather and listen to the same opera performed live on multiple different occasions, each time straining to hear whether their favorite soprano or tenor had what it took to hit the high notes that night. With the slightest hint of pride in his voice, Gelb said that the Met's movie theater broadcasts have, in the 21st century, become the performing arts equivalent of Monday Night

Football: "It's a sports-like, gladiatorial experience listening to live opera."[12]

Launched in the 2006–2007 season, the *Live in HD* broadcasts are filmed by 10 to 12 HD cameras installed on and around the Met's stage. The camera locations are specially chosen for each production, with the cameras never permanently installed, allowing the program to keep abreast of the cutting edge in high-definition technology. The camera angles provide unique views of the singers and the scenery, and Gelb himself produces the broadcasts from a van parked outside the opera house, tweaking the lighting and the camera angles in real time for best effect. Critics have said that the presence of TV cameras has affected the way the Met designs its productions, tailoring them for screens rather than the stage. Gelb refuted this: "Despite what's been written in the *New Yorker* and elsewhere, I never tell stage directors to think for the camera. The Met is a live performance venue, not a soundstage. We might adjust the lighting by 10 percent here and there to make sure that certain things work on camera. It is the same thing the people in the audience are seeing. Well, as long as the original lighting designer isn't there to see it."[13]

The broadcasts have drastically increased the number of people who can experience the Met's performances. In the 2012–2013 season, 12 operas were broadcast to 1,900 movie theaters in 60 countries.[14] Even if the Met sold out all of its performances in a given season, which it does not, that would mean that a total of only 700,000 people in the house seats were able to experience the productions.[15] Global viewership of the broadcasts in 2012 was 2.5 million.[16]

Despite initial fears that the *Live in HD* broadcasts would be a loss leader, the series proved profitable by its third season and currently contributes about $17 million annually to the Met's bottom line.[17]

During Gelb's presentation, a student asked whether the broadcasts have diverted ticket sales away from live opera in places outside New York City. Gelb said he didn't think so and pointed out that the Met does only around ten broadcasts per year, a number that most likely whets local appetite for live opera without satisfying it. And cultivating a live audience in an age when time-shifted media consumption is growing is the key to having a vibrant, distinctive place for the performing arts in the future media landscape, said Gelb.

The Met's technology strategy also includes a Sirius XM radio channel launched in 2006, a first for the opera world, and an online subscription service, which gives users access to a complete archive of filmed Met operas as well as the live broadcasts, which are put online several months after their initial transmission.[18]

Harnessing new technology rather than seeing it as a threat to a live art form comes naturally to Gelb because of his background in the recording industry. It was actually a David Bowie live promotion created by Sony's pop music division and linked with movie theaters that Gelb witnessed during his time at Sony Classical that first gave him the idea to create the Met's *Live in HD* broadcasts.[19]

INCREASING ARTS EDUCATION

Gelb believes that the waning interest in opera on the part of younger people comes from a lack of education about it, not any flaw in the art form itself. Under his tenure, the Met has vastly increased its educational outreach efforts, especially online. In an age of slashed government education budgets, almost all opera education in America now comes from opera companies themselves. It is Gelb's hope that as more young people are introduced to opera, it will lose its reputation as either a boring or elitist activity.

REVIVING THE THEATRICALITY OF MET PRODUCTIONS

Nobody would argue that the Met has ever been lacking musically, but when Gelb came on board, it had come to be seen as an artistically stifling place for directors and designers. The acting style was known colloquially as "park and bark," meaning that little more was expected of singers than that they hit their mark on the stage and belt out the right notes. The string of theater and film directors whom Gelb has hired at the Met in recent years has changed that standard not only on the stage at Lincoln Center (where the Met is located) but on opera stages around the world.

It is now no longer enough for up-and-coming singers to have beautiful voices. They have to be able to act, too. One of the darlings of the Met's stage in recent years, Jonas Kaufmann, is often praised in the press for his acting skills as much as his voice.

Gelb has also set about commissioning more new productions, an average of six each season, with each season opener being a brand-new production. His recruited directors have included big names from outside opera, like the late British film director Anthony Minghella, South African artist William Kentridge, and American playwright and theater director Mary Zimmerman. Gelb says he made a point of finding directors who would come to opera with a fresh eye or who had previously shied away from the Met.[20]

Gelb doesn't see his flashier new productions as a departure from the true faith, as many do, but rather a return to it. He points out that opera's great strength has always been that it uses all of the arts at once: "visually stunning sets, emotionally moving acting and storytelling, and, of course, transcendent music."[21]

COMMUNITY ENGAGEMENT

Gelb had a piece of advice for students that is applicable to an arts organization of any kind and size: Engage with the community and recognize that you don't operate in a vacuum. Find other organizations that you can partner with so that you can boost one another's attendance and profile.

In the Met's case, that means peer organizations like New York's Museum of Modern Art (MoMA), the New York Public Library, and the Guggenheim Museum. A 2010 MoMA exhibition of works by William Kentridge coincided with the 2010 premiere at the Met of Shostakovich's opera *The Nose*, whose production design was done entirely by Kentridge. The synergy was no accident, but was planned years in advance by Gelb and MoMA's director, Glenn Lowry. As Gelb tells it, the idea cropped up as the two were sharing a meal—proof that it is beneficial to reach out to other arts leaders in your community even with no specific goal in mind.

If you can't find anything going on in your community, Gelb advised that students create a cross-media event of their own, like he did for the Met's *Prince Igor*. In a section of the Met's lobby that had not been used as an art gallery before, Gelb mounted a multimedia exhibit depicting multiple imaginings of what Prince Igor, a real figure from medieval Russian history, might have looked like.

———

Throughout Gelb's long run of controversial decisions, the Met's board of directors has supported him, especially during the labor negotiations of the summer of 2014, the Met's most intense in three decades. Dragging on for the entire summer, the negotiations avoided a general strike (and thus a delay in the Met's season, which actually happened in 1980) only at the last minute after several all-night bargaining sessions.[22]

During his tenure, Gelb has managed to attract record donations. Met board chair Ann Ziff and her family have given more than $65 million since 2006, including a single gift of $30 million, the largest in the opera house's history.[23]

But before the record donations and even the job itself came Gelb's courage to speak his mind. Referring to his initial job interview, Gelb said, "I was hired based on that critique. I was hired because I could apply real-life knowledge to an organization that had become disconnected from everyday life."[24]

"My chief goal," he said, "is to help keep the art form alive and the Met alive in the future."[25]

SIR CLIVE GILLINSON, EXECUTIVE AND ARTISTIC DIRECTOR, CARNEGIE HALL

FOUR REASONS TO GIVE YOUR PRODUCT AWAY FOR FREE

Carnegie Hall is the most famous concert hall in the world. Its name is so widely known that when Sir Clive Gillinson left his job as manager of the London Symphony Orchestra to head up Carnegie Hall in 2005, he got a call from the *Bangalore Times*. Gillinson was born in Bangalore, India, but lived only the first three months of his life there. That didn't stop the paper from running the front-page headline "Bangalore Boy Takes Over Carnegie Hall." During his tenure, he has transformed the flagship concert venue into a beacon of arts education and outreach. When he spoke to the students of "Understanding the Profession: The Performing Arts in the 21st Century," he was adamant that not-for-profit arts organizations shouldn't be afraid to give their resources away for free. Here are his four reasons.

1. It keeps you close to your values. Arts organizations in general and not-for-profit arts organizations in particular don't gain their power in society because of their wealth. They gain it because of the values they are dedicated to. When you are willing to give your product away for free, it forces you to have a compelling answer to the key questions: "Why are we doing this? Why does our organization exist?" When you're not working for financial rewards, you have to be very clear about your mission to stay motivated.

In the case of Gillinson and Carnegie Hall, his answer to both questions comes from a clear and unwavering dedication to the inherent value of music. Says Gillinson, "Our responsibility is to the future of music and the impact it can have on people's lives."

2. It changes your relationship to your audience. When somebody exchanges money for a product or an experience, they are a customer. When somebody is offered a product or an experience for free, they are the recipient of a gift. Giving your product away for free can transform and enrich the public's relationship to your organization by making people patrons and partners rather than mere customers. Gillinson sees those who are the beneficiaries of Carnegie Hall's education and outreach programs as no less than "partners in the future of music."

3. It makes it much easier to raise money. Imagine yourself approaching a potential donor. You have two possible pitches. The first is, "We are doing our best to monetize our product, but we cannot possibly charge enough to make ourselves profitable. Can you help make up the difference?" The second pitch is, "We are making our art and our educational resources available for free to the community and the world. Can you help us make that possible?" Gillinson believes that the second pitch is by far the more inspiring of the two. Too many arts institutions, he believes, waste time trying to figure out how to monetize what they do. The result is that they end up not making very much money and also not making much of a difference. Donors want to give to projects with a clearly defined higher purpose. When you are giving away great art, nobody has any doubt about what that purpose is.

4. It increases the impact of your organization. The people who need your art most might not be able to afford it. It is too often the people on society's margins who lack the experiences, hope, and meaning that great art can offer them. When you give away what you do, you have a better chance of making a difference where it matters most.

Carnegie Hall's outreach and education programs, transformed and greatly expanded under Gillinson's tenure, are a great example of this philosophy in action. The programs now reach about 450,000 people per year, in the form of extensive educational programs in schools and free performances and classes in hospitals, homeless shelters, senior centers, and prisons.[26] A program called Musical Connections offers long-term musical instruction to juveniles and adults in the prison system, including inmates at Sing Sing in New York State.

Sing Sing is one of the most notorious prisons in the world, with 79 percent of its inmates having been convicted of a violent crime, and over half locked up for ten years or more.[27] Carnegie Hall's outreach program engages a group of highly trained musicians to lead a selection of inmates in a year-long composition workshop that culminates in an end-of-year concert. At the concert, an ensemble made up of the inmates and musicians from Carnegie Hall play a program that includes original works composed by the inmates themselves.

Musical Connections aims to help transform the inmates into people capable of reintegrating into society once they are outside the prison walls. It also aims to lift some of the soul-crushing burden of incarceration.

Gillinson felt the impact of the program at Sing Sing when he attended one of the program's end-of-year concerts. There were 90 inmates in the audience, and Gillinson said he'd never seen a group more attentive, silent, and totally absorbed in the music. After the performance, he asked one of the participants what the project had meant to him. He received a baffled look in return; then the inmate said, "This isn't just a project. This is my life."[28] Speaking of the program's impact on his life, another inmate remarked, "The bars, the cells, this location, it no longer exists. It's just me and the music and how I feel inside."[29]

Transformative power like that is truly something you cannot put a price tag on.

MEREDITH "MAX" HODGES, FORMER EXECUTIVE DIRECTOR, GALLIM DANCE

THE POWER OF PLANNED GROWTH

About halfway through her presentation to the students of "Understanding the Profession: The Performing Arts in the 21st Century," Meredith "Max" Hodges unveiled her secret weapon, the Opportunity Framework. It's a method for making decisions that she learned from Alan Grossman, one of her Harvard Business School professors. She says it helped her nearly double the budget of Gallim Dance in the two years after she joined the company as its executive director in 2012. (Hodges joined the Boston Ballet in 2014, as we discuss later.)

The Opportunity Framework was designed to solve the biggest problem facing all not-for-profits: how to stay afloat financially while fulfilling an organization's core mission. The Framework depends on a big-picture, long-term view of an organization's mission and all its activities, but it is also capable of delivering a solid answer to the more tactical question "What do I do first on a busy Monday morning?"

THE OPPORTUNITY FRAMEWORK

The Opportunity Framework is plotted on an x-y axis similar to one you'd find in an algebra textbook. The x-axis runs horizontally, with mission fulfillment increasing as you move from left to right (Figure 6-1). On the far left are activities that don't fulfill the mission, while on the far right are activities that do. The y-axis runs vertically, with profitability increasing as you move upward. Activities that deposit money

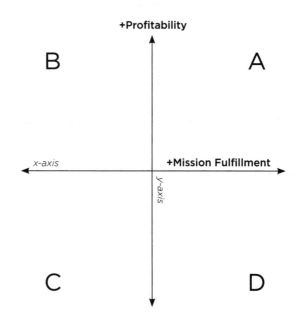

Figure 6-1. The Opportunity Framework. *Adapted with permission of Meredith Hodges. Opportunity Framework used with permission of Dr. Alan Grossman.*

in the bank are at the top, while activities that drain money are at the bottom.

The upper right quadrant (A) combines mission fulfillment and profitability. In an ideal world, it's where all your activities would be. For a not-for-profit, this quadrant is the sweet spot. You want to put as much of your activity here as possible, says Hodges.

The upper left quadrant (B) is for activities that turn a profit but don't necessarily fulfill the organization's mission. During Hodges's presentation, one Juilliard student identified this quadrant as "selling out," and Hodges smiled and nodded her head, adding that some activities in this spot are inevitable for any nonprofit. The trick is to accept projects with very strong profit margins, especially if they provide a quick turnaround. The catch is twofold. First, avoid projects that, while profitable, might eat up too much time. "It it's going to take up, say, one day a week for the next 11 weeks, then it's an automatic *no*," Hodges told the students.[30] The other catch is to avoid any projects that actively contradict or inhibit your mission.

The lower left quadrant (C) combines mission failure and money loss. Anything you're already doing that shows up here should be dropped as quickly as possible, and any optional new projects that could be plotted here should be avoided. It might seem obvious to ditch activities in this quadrant, but until you think in terms of the Opportunity Framework, it might not be obvious what is actually a drain on mission and money. Hodges emphasized to the students the need to be ruthlessly honest about which activities fall into this quadrant: "It doesn't matter if they are services you need to provide. You find another way."[31] For example, programs that benefit deserving recipients but are outside your own organization's mission might be transferred to a partner, ideally one with more competency in the program area. Services your audience or visitors might need, like running a museum café (see below), can be maintained but moved out of this quadrant by outsourcing them or changing the way you achieve them, usually by seeing how a peer organization has solved the problem and emulating its actions.

The lower right quadrant (D) is for those activities that fulfill your mission but don't make money. Supporting activity in this quadrant is the reason not-for-profits exist—or, as Hodges quips at her own expense, "Losing money but fulfilling your mission: the definition of contemporary dance!"[32] For anything that falls into this quadrant, the plan is simple: Pursue as many projects as can be funded.

While she was Gallim's director, Hodges and her staff made daily use of the Opportunity Framework to choose a portfolio of projects to work on and decide which ones needed attention and when. They used it to plan out not only what they were going to do on any given day but also what to put on Gallim's long-term schedule. Though Hodges says she often had fun applying the Framework, she never lost sight of how high the stakes were: "Our goal is to spend every dollar and every hour of our staff's time that we can afford to spend on fulfilling the mission of the organization. And so, how do you do that?"[33]

At first glance, the Juilliard and Fordham students were wary of the Framework. To a roomful of artists, using an x-y axis to set your priorities seemed stilted, and one or two raised their hands to say so. But, after Hodges plotted a few examples from Gallim's real-world activities, the power of the Framework quickly become evident. It revealed itself as a tool for refining intuition, not stifling it (see Figure 6-2).

Gallim's stated mission is "creating and performing original work by Andrea Miller [its founder], nurturing the careers of young artists, and stimulating the imagination of a diverse international audience." Keeping Gallim's mission in mind, Hodges plotted four examples on the Opportunity Framework and explained their placement:

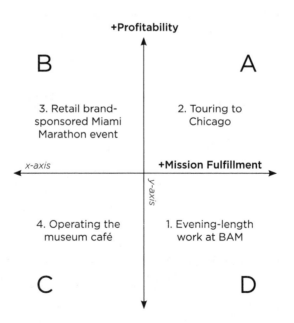

Figure 6-2. The Opportunity Framework in action. *Adapted with permission of Meredith Hodges. Opportunity Framework used with permission of Dr. Alan Grossman.*

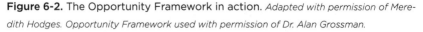

1. Creating a new evening-length work and performing its world premiere at the Brooklyn Academy of Music (BAM) It is the huge cost, in both time and money, of creating a new work that puts this activity firmly in the lower right quadrant of the Framework rather than the upper right. It fulfills Gallim's mission perfectly, but it cannot possibly be profitable. It takes Miller and her dancers about 20 weeks of regular time in Gallim's studio to create a new work. That is almost half of the 44 weeks out of each year that the company's dancers are paid to be active. Then, there are payments to the composer for the score and to the musicians who will record it, as well as fees paid to lighting and costume designers, etc. Hodges explains that BAM, though a world-class institution and a great partner, cannot reasonably be expected to pay a fee high enough or generate enough ticket sales to offset the creation of a new work. So she plots this in the lower right, Quadrant D.

2. Touring to Chicago When performing arts companies travel, they are paid a flat fee by the venue that invites them to perform. Touring groups can end up with a profit after their hotel and travel expenses are subtracted from this flat fee. It's not always a huge amount, but because the flat fee is known in advance, many tours can be planned to ensure a profit. For Gallim, it is especially beneficial to travel to Europe, where state-funded arts venues can afford fees that are generous in comparison to those paid by most venues in the United States. As Hodges put it, "We love going to Paris."[34] Touring to Chicago, too, is profitable enough to warrant being placed in Quadrant A.

3. Performing at a Miami Marathon event Gallim danced at the 2013 Miami Marathon while wearing a major retail brand's latest line of sportswear. Gallim's only direct expenses were airfare and per diems for the dancers, all offset by the substantial fee paid by the brand, which was accustomed to paying the fees of creatives in the commercial advertising world—on average much higher than those in the performing arts world. To the students, Hodges said the "revenue for that gig was really great," which puts it at the top of Quadrant B. The caveat here, she warned again, is to watch out for profitable activities that suck up too much staff time to make it worthwhile.[35]

4. Operating the museum café For her final example, Hodges drew on her experience in the museum world. A gift shop or a café might seem like a ready win for a nonprofit, but it can quickly turn into both a money pit and a time waster. Said Hodges, "Running a restaurant profitably is a hard thing that people specialize in and spend their whole lives trying to get right, and it turns out that museum curators may not be good at it."[36] So the activity goes into Quadrant C, a distraction from the mission and a money loser.

The way to flip this particular activity from Quadrant C to Quadrant B is to do what most big cultural institutions do: collect a fee from an established name in the restaurant business in exchange for letting it use prime museum real estate. Even if the fee were as low as $10 a year, it would still be better than losing money on a non-mission activity.

Hodges and her team applied this tactic to the use of their Brooklyn studio space. Rather than letting the space go unused when the company was not rehearsing or teaching their own movement classes, Miller and Hodges decided to offer additional classes in yoga and African dance. In addition to making productive use of the space, it also raised Gallim's profile in the community. And rather than offer the classes themselves, something Gallim was not necessarily prepared to do, they found established yoga and African dance instructors with existing clientele who were willing to pay the company a nominal fee for the use of the space. Gallim's profit margin for the classes wasn't very high, but it was still a stream of revenue that didn't exist previously, and it didn't demand expertise that Gallim didn't already have.

When applying the Framework, or thinking more abstractly about future activities, it is important not just to think passively. Said Hodges, "If somebody calls and offers you an opportunity in Quadrant A, of course you say yes. But what else do you do? You spend your days pursuing new and additional opportunities that land in that quadrant."[37] Don't just classify existing opportunities, but use the Framework to imagine and implement new ones.

A sense of balance is also important to success. Loading up all your activity in just one of the three desirable quadrants won't lead to success, said Hodges. You need to pursue a balanced portfolio of activity across all three desirable quadrants: A, B, and D.

THE OPPORTUNITY FRAMEWORK'S IMPACT ON GALLIM

During Hodges's tenure, Gallim underwent a period of explosive growth. Founded in 2007 by its artistic director, Andrea Miller, just two years after her graduation from Juilliard, the company was started with enormous ambition but modest means. Its first rehearsal spaces were Juilliard classrooms that she and the dancers would sneak into after hours. Their first gigs were all money losers, where they paid for the privilege of performing in venues where they had a shot at being noticed by presenters and agents. Miller's mother donated enough so the dancers could be paid $50 per performance. The whole operation was run out of Miller's apartment, with dancers doing all the administrative work in their spare hours.[38]

Hodges first encountered Gallim in 2010 at Fall for Dance, an annual event held at New York City Center, a performance venue in Manhattan. The lineup at Fall for Dance is designed to be a mix of names you know and some you haven't heard of yet. At that time, Gallim was one of the unknowns. Hodges was impressed by two things. The first was Gallim's stellar performance, which convinced her that the group had a bright artistic future. The second was Miller's performance with the donors and dance patrons sitting in the first few rows of the audience. Rather than hanging back after the show and relying on her dancers' performance alone to shine for her, Miller was out in the crowd shaking hands and making connections. These patrons, some of whom became Gallim's most valued trustees, appreciated how bold Miller was in talking about Gallim's budget, the small size of which astonished them.

By 2012, five years after its founding, Hodges was brought on board as Gallim's first executive director. Her role was to direct the business operations, as Miller directed the artistic vision and choreography. In the 2012–2013 season, the first year of Hodges's stewardship, Gallim's budget grew from $414,000 to $699,000, a huge leap of 68 percent.[39] Hodges attributes the change to having a plan for growth, informed daily by the Opportunity Framework: "We moved to a phase where we were planning ahead, setting goals, and stretching ourselves, not just picking up the phone and accepting whatever was coming in." The growth continued after that first year. Gallim's revenue in 2013 was $761,000, a solid 8 percent increase on the previous year.[40]

To the students of "Understanding the Profession: The Performing Arts in the 21st Century," Hodges stated her bold objective: "to grow Gallim to be one of the biggies." By biggies, she meant established modern dance companies like the Paul Taylor Dance Company, which has an average annual budget of $8 million.[41]

After two years with Hodges at the helm as executive director and continued artistic excellence by Miller, Gallim is on solid footing. It now occupies a permanent location in Brooklyn with offices and rehearsal space, and it employs seven full-time dancers, with 44 weeks of paid activity per year, more than most dance companies. Miller's ambitious choreography has been recognized with a Guggenheim Fellowship, a tremendous honor for a young artist.[42]

Hodges's presence at Gallim was a testament to the fact that even the most exceptional art needs the help of a good business sense to survive. Hodges said, of her business school education as it applied to the art world: "It 100 percent translated. Every single moment of my education translated. I think it's unfair to assume people need lessons to play the violin but running an organization should just be intuitive."[43]

THE POWER OF PLANNED GROWTH IN HODGES'S CAREER

Hodges has applied the same careful strategies for growth to her own future as well as Gallim's. As early as her business school days, she set herself on a direct path to where she is today. "I wanted to be the executive director of a cultural organization," Hodges said. "I couldn't have told you for sure it was going to be a dance organization, but I would have said for sure it was a nonprofit."[44] While she was an MBA student, Hodges wrote, "More people need art: the thick, anguished brush strokes of a Van Gogh; the high soaring notes of an overture; the whisper and promise of an opening curtain."[45] That sense of mission has been driving her ever since.

After completing her Harvard BA and MBA (both with honors), Hodges went on to work at Bain & Company, which regularly jostles with McKinsey for the top spot among the world's consulting firms. Even though she could have gone from Bain to just about anywhere in the business world, she stuck to her plan to be of service to the arts.

Her first stop in the art world was in the finance department of the Museum of Modern Art. Trading high finance for high art meant taking a serious pay cut, but Hodges said it has been worth it. After making a meaningful contribution and learning some great lessons at MoMA, she was ready to make a deliberate move to a smaller organization. She wanted to go from the middle tier of a large, established cultural institution to the top tier of a small one, where her efforts would make a more noticeable difference.

She recommends a similar strategy to anybody who wants to follow in her footsteps. Start at a blue-chip organization, which will give you both credibility and a great knowledge base, and then branch out to a place where your efforts not only result in bigger changes but can also get you noticed more easily. While Hodges is too modest to say so, it's obvious that she is on track to be running a place like Lincoln Center in 20 years' time.

In 2014, Hodges was tapped by the Boston Ballet as its next executive director. With an annual budget of about $30 million,[46] cultural prestige as New England's oldest professional ballet company, and the largest ballet school in North America, it no doubt represents Hodges's first but confident steps onto a much larger stage.

RACHEL S. MOORE, FORMER CHIEF EXECUTIVE OFFICER, AMERICAN BALLET THEATRE

BRANDING

The "Beleaguered American Ballet Theatre" In 2006, during her second year as the administrative head of American Ballet Theatre (ABT), Rachel S. Moore found herself traveling back and forth to Washington, D.C., to meet with senators and members of the House of Representatives. It was a surreal experience for her and an unusual one for the head of a ballet company. She was in Washington trying to complete the final stages of a lobbying campaign that was also a rebranding campaign. Her goal was to get Congress to pass a bill declaring ABT the official ballet company of the United States. It was a move typical of Moore's management style: adventurous but also part of a rational, long-term strategy.

Moore's focus on branding and her path to Washington began before she was even hired as ABT's administrative head. As part of the interview process a year earlier, she had found herself sitting across from ABT's then board chair Lewis Ranieri, a formidable Wall Street figure who was profiled in Michael Lewis's history of 1980s high finance, *Liar's Poker*. At issue was an ABT ad campaign, then on the streets, which Moore felt contained awkward language and a heroin chic aesthetic that was in poor taste and didn't reflect ABT's identity. She couldn't have known that Ranieri had spearheaded and signed off on the ads himself. Despite Ranieri's gall at her criticism (he later joked that he narrowly restrained himself from "throttling" her), he and the rest of the board eventually voted Moore into ABT's top administrative job.

The board had been looking for a candidate with a different profile. They wanted a hardened administrative veteran at the end of his career who could tackle the numerous internal threats to ABT's existence. Instead, they ended up choosing Moore, then just entering mid-career, because of her vision and her deep connections to ABT itself.

Moore had first studied ballet at the age of 11 in California's rural Central Valley. Just a few years after taking up ballet, she found herself commuting to Sacramento to study at the ballet there, and by 16 she was spending summers at ABT in New York. At 18, she became a full-fledged member of ABT's corps de ballet, led by none other than Mikhail Baryshnikov (or "Misha," as she calls him). Though a broken ankle ended her dance career when she was just 24, Moore pivoted quickly to another path and managed to successfully apply to college, graduating Phi Beta Kappa from Brown University, despite being seven years out of step with her peers.

During her summers away from Brown, she interned at the National Endowment for the Arts in Washington, D.C., where she was the congressional liaison. Her time at the NEA piqued her interest in arts policy and helped her be open to later study at Columbia University, where she earned an MA in arts administration. Throughout it all, she never lost her strong emotional connection to ballet, which she says formed the core of her developing personality as an adolescent. After a slate of increasingly prestigious jobs in dance administration, including two positions at the Boston Ballet during a time of crisis for the company, Moore was ready to step in and help ABT in its own time of crisis.

She jokes that before her tenure, the press had a disconcerting epithet for ABT: the "beleaguered American Ballet Theatre." At an institution where cash flow is intermittent (Moore calls it "lumpy") at the best of times, things were so bad when she started as head of ABT that the dancers and musicians were barely getting paid on time. Partly responsible for this was the fact that ABT's longtime mainstay, its touring business, had faltered, and top-level management was turning over so quickly that nothing was being done about it. Added to that was a board of directors that was seen to have drifted from a clear understanding of its core responsibilities and that had forgotten where its responsibilities differed from that of the full-time staff.[47]

Underlying all these difficulties, as Moore saw it, was a branding problem. Even before taking the reins as ABT's executive director, she knew that balancing the books and reinvigorating the staff were not going to be enough to turn things around. Before making progress, she and the company needed to answer a vital question: What was ABT's core identity?

America's National Ballet Company Another name for a branding problem is an identity crisis. At its worst, rebranding is a series of superficial changes made to a company's public image meant to mislead people. At its best, rebranding can help a company answer the question "Who are we and what is our purpose?" No company or even person can entirely escape the branding problem. We all have an image that the outside world sees and, like it or not, even choosing not to care about this fact is still a branding choice. The ancient Greek philosopher Socrates understood something of branding when he advised his ambitious pupils to "be that which you wish to seem." He was saying, in other words, that a change of perception—both how others see us and how we see ourselves—can translate into a change of being.

In the context of the marketplace, the most urgent question of branding is how to be different from other companies or people who supply the same product. How certain companies have solved this problem has resulted in some icons of daily American life. Coca-Cola needed a way to let its drinkers know why its formula was best. Apple, in its famous 1984 Super Bowl ad, told the world how it was different from IBM, and the world has never forgotten. Strip away Coke's black-and-red color scheme and tagline ("The real thing") or Apple's logos and slogan ("Think different"), and you'd have nothing but undifferentiated bottles of carbonated sugar water or boxes of circuitry. No matter how good a product may be, without its brand identifier, the experience of using it isn't quite the same. The ideas and emotions tied to some brand names are an intangible but essential part of a product.

In the case of ABT, it needed to differentiate itself from its main competitor, New York City Ballet (NYCB). Both companies had been founded in the 1940s and were headquartered in Manhattan. Both have world-class reputations as producers and performers of ballet. But while most New Yorkers thought of NYCB as a hometown institution worth buying high-price tickets for and cutting big donation checks to, they didn't see ABT in the same way.

There was good reason for this. ABT had long been a touring company that spent most of its season away from New York. While it often performs on the Lincoln Center campus, ABT doesn't have a permanent space there, like NYCB's Koch Theater, which is just across the plaza from the permanent homes of the New York Philharmonic and the Metropolitan Opera. In fact, ABT doesn't have a permanent performance space anywhere in New York City. But despite its long touring season, no place outside New York City felt that ABT was part of its community, either.

When she was hired, Moore said that even at ABT itself nobody had a strong sense of where the company belonged, and that this in turn weakened the sense of mission and pride that all not-for-profit staffs rely on as their daily fuel. "We needed to reframe ourselves from a vision/mission viewpoint, but also in a way that strengthened the business case," says Moore.[48]

As a starting point, Moore reached back to a previous rebranding effort that had been made by none other than President Dwight D. Eisenhower. In 1957, Eisenhower called for ABT's name to be changed from Ballet Theatre to American Ballet Theatre, so that the company could tour behind the Iron Curtain as a symbol of American cultural vibrancy. At the time, the U.S. government was giving money and clout to other artistic institutions, like MoMA, which mounted international traveling exhibitions of abstract expressionist painting. It was all part of a strategy to project American soft power in the global struggle for dominance with the Soviets.

During the Cold War, ABT traveled the world via military aircraft and found itself coming into contact with ambassadors and heads of state. Upon meeting some members of the company, Soviet premier Nikita Khrushchev quipped, "How can these people be so thin if they are from the land of milk and honey?" ABT's role as an official cultural ambassador continued throughout the 1950s, 1960s, and 1970s.

Moore, knowing this lore from her days in ABT's corps, was inspired to once again cast the company as America's national ballet, putting it in league with the great national companies of Europe like the Paris Opera Ballet and England's Royal Ballet. This would differentiate ABT from NYCB, while also giving it a boost in prestige.

Moore and her team set about formulating a tagline, which is a necessary element in the creation of any brand. A tagline is a short, memorable phrase that sums up a brand identity and makes it stick in the mind. Some familiar ones are Maxwell House Coffee's "Good to the last drop," American Express's "Don't leave home without it," and "Like a good neighbor, State Farm is there." Moore and her team settled on "American Ballet Theatre, bringing dance to America and American dance to the world." It was when she overheard one of her ballerinas making fun of the phrase that she knew the idea was good: "I thought, 'Yay! Snark!' When the staff starts making fun of it, you know the idea is entrenched."[49]

Moore says the rebranding reenergized the staff. They no longer worked at "the Beleaguered American Ballet Theatre," but at an organization that was out to change the world. Throughout the company, people started feeling once again that they had an occasion to rise to. ABT's new identity became the center of a web of changes that spread throughout the company, bringing a renewed energy and positive outlook with it.

Not satisfied with just self-definition as America's national ballet, Moore decided to complete what Eisenhower had started and get an official stamp of approval from the federal government. Like any business that wants to get in touch with its congressional representatives, Moore and her team hired a lobbyist. After wrangling with senators and representatives (some of whom knew almost nothing about the arts) and engaging in some "good old-fashioned Washington horse trading,"[50] as she puts it, Moore found herself with bipartisan sponsorship of a joint resolution in the Senate and the House. The bill was passed and in 2006, ABT officially became "America's National Ballet Company."[51]

Touring The first immediate benefit of the federal government's imprimatur was a reinvigoration of ABT's international touring business. Europe's national companies are most comfortable partnering with an organization they see as a direct peer. ABT, with its congressionally approved status, now officially fits that bill.

ABT has also resumed its work with the State Department and once again represents the United States abroad. Off the top of her head, Moore mentions touring to Cuba and Abu Dhabi in the United Arab Emirates, and being the first American performing arts organization to perform in Oman, which flew in the Dresden Philharmonic to play for the dancers and mark the occasion.

In the course of proving its national status, ABT had offered evidence to Congress that throughout its history it had performed in all 50 states. And in keeping with its tagline, "Bringing dance to America," ABT has hit the road again in earnest throughout the United States.

As with all the fine performing arts, the audience around the country for ballet is declining, but Moore has a brand-based solution for that as well. By lending ABT certification to dance schools throughout America, Moore and company hope not only to improve the quality of dance education but to educate the next generation about the value of classical dance as a cultural activity.

The Kleenex of the Ballet World In her office near Union Square in Manhattan, Moore gets up from the interview table to pull one of a series of thick binders off the shelf. Full to the brim with glossy pages separated by colorful tabs, the binder is one volume in ABT's extensive guide for dance teachers. "Education," says Moore with a chuckle, "is part of the perfect cradle-to-grave marketing strategy."[52]

Moore is the first executive in ABT's history to launch a comprehensive dance education initiative. She is familiar with how healing and also how harmful dance education can be for young people. When she encountered ballet at age 11, she found learning it to be a bastion of grace and rationality in her life, and it helped her build a strong sense of self. But inside ballet's brutal meritocracy, it is impossible that every young dancer will overcome all the challenges set before them. Normal adolescent and teenage feelings of inadequacy or troubled body image can become exaggerated when judgment of the dancer in the classroom is confused with judgment of the person outside the classroom.

ABT's branded curriculum is designed to help prevent such potential harm to young dancers by tempering instructional attitudes and methods. "We want to avoid a situation where students are living in terror," says Moore, "which is no way to create a healthy artist or a healthy human being." Moore says she cried every night as an ABT summer student and was probably not the only ballerina to do so. Some students are so traumatized by the ballet instruction process that they abandon dance altogether, even as future audience members. Says Moore: "I have many friends who will not even walk into a theater after training for ten years as a dancer. And that's lamentable."[53] It is also the exact opposite of one objective of Moore's educational initiative: the creation of a future audience for ballet.

When local dance teachers become certified in ABT's curriculum, they are allowed to put ABT's logo on their place of business and on their promotional materials. Moore thinks of it as something like the *Good Housekeeping* "Seal of Approval." This promotes good instruction by giving ABT-certified teachers a marketing edge against their competitors, and it also leads to successive classes of students who are used to associating their own dance education with the institution of ABT itself.

Teachers maintain their certification by presenting their students for examination once every two years to ABT-appointed examiners. The examiners also provide in-class feedback to the instructors, which Moore says most dance teachers are desperate for. There are currently 1,400 teachers of the ABT curriculum in 48 states and 13 countries.[54] The curriculum has even secured a beachhead in St. Petersburg, Russia, home to that formidable fortress of Russian ballet, the Vaganova

Academy. Moore hopes that the ABT curriculum will further reinforce abroad the idea of a distinctive American style of ballet.

Moore sets aside the binder and pulls out a pair of tiny pink ballet shoes. The ABT logo is stamped onto the leather soles, and a black-and-white picture of an ABT ballerina appears on the box. The shoes are offered at Payless, and Moore says about 1.2 million pairs are sold each year. The partnership began through a longtime member of ABT's board, a former Payless CEO.[55]

ABT also sells branded leotards, which the company contracted out from two leading manufacturers, first Capezio and now IDS. All the students in ABT-certified schools wear ABT-branded garments, which helps not only with revenue generation but with further identification by the students between ABT and excellence in ballet.

"We want to become the Kleenex of the ballet world," says Moore. Kleenex, while still an official brand name, has become so identified with its products that it is used interchangeably as a noun for tissue.[56]

All of this adds up not only to a solid and stable source of revenue for ABT but also a foothold for ballet in the economic life of America. "The last thing a parent is going to give up in tough times is something that's good for their children," says Moore. Far from viewing it as a coldhearted ploy, Moore sees ABT's integration into dance education as a way for the company to advance its values. When all the arts are part of education, it becomes much harder to see them as just luxuries. They become part of what it means to grow into a fully realized human being.[57]

National Brand, National Revenue While the official stamp of congressional approval did not bring any federal money, it did give ABT access to new sources of revenue. In the world of corporate sponsorships, there are separate pots of money that companies set aside for regional and for national campaigns. Most organizations get a shot at only one of them. But ABT, since it regularly puts on performances in regional centers while also maintaining a national presence, is often in the running for both types of funding.

The justification for this, according to Moore, is that individuals with high net worth, whose attention is so valued by corporate marketing departments, are likely to bring their knowledge of ABT's brand with them as they travel around the country. ABT is a consistent presence in Palm Beach, on Rodeo Drive, and on Broadway.

To relieve some of the pressure that comes from competing with NYCB for board members and their contributions, ABT has moved its annual *Nutcracker* from New York City to Orange County, California, where it also plans to establish a school. Orange County, which has the third highest concentration of millionaires of any U.S. county, has no resident ballet company.[58] Moore very much hopes that ABT will fill the vacuum. She hopes an annual *Nutcracker* will give ABT an entry to being seen as a part of the local community. When an Orange County resident writes a check big enough to win him a spot on ABT's board, Moore wants him to honestly feel that he is giving back to the place where he lives.

GIVING BALLET A STRONGER FUTURE

Largely white, wealthy, and conservative Orange County is not the only new community where ABT hopes to make itself better known. In minority communities across America, ballet—where it is known at all—is often seen as remote and elitist. Moore thinks of this not just as an identity crisis for ABT but for ballet itself. She points out that in 2014, there were still no African-American principal ballet dancers anywhere in America, or in any major ballet company in the world.[59]

Moore is very proud of ABT's Misty Copeland (then soloist, now prima ballerina as of summer 2015), whose memoir *Life in Motion: An*

Unlikely Ballerina is about, among other things, being a black dancer in the nearly monolithically white ballet world. Copeland's memoir hit the *New York Times* bestseller list in 2014, and she is universally seen as a prodigy in the dance world. She is only the third African-American ballerina in ABT's history. Copeland's success is a cause for joy, says Moore, but it doesn't mean that both ABT and ballet don't have a long, long way to go.

Bringing more diversity to dance is morally right, but Moore also points out that it's a good long-term business move for all ballet companies. As America moves toward a future where whites will be a minority sometime around mid-century, unless ballet reaches out to nonwhite communities, it may someday find itself without an audience of meaningful size.

To this end, ABT under Moore's leadership founded Project Plié, an educational initiative whose explicit goal is to diversify America's ballet companies. Partnering with the Boys and Girls Clubs of America, Project Plié introduces students to ballet through performance and instruction, and also seeks to identify future talent. And though she doesn't say so, it's easy to imagine Moore being quite pleased if the future dancers and audience members of Project Plié grow up with a strong association between ballet and ABT's brand.

Giving ballet a future is not just part of Moore's job description—it's a mission that gives her daily strength: "People before me worked hard to give me my chance. I feel it's my obligation to do the same for future dancers."

Starting in the fall of 2015, Moore will assume leadership of the Music Center in Los Angeles, which houses the Los Angeles Philharmonic, the Los Angeles Opera, Center Theatre Group, and the Los Angeles Master Chorale.[60]

★ ★ **KEYNOTES** ★ ★

Questions to Ask Yourself

- Am I making full use of technology to promote my organization or bring my performances to as many people as possible?
- Can I link up my mission and activities to performing arts education? (Besides being a great way to enrich the lives of young people and create future audiences for the performing arts, adding an educational component to your mission can make you or your organization eligible for a host of private and public grants.)
- Are there any other artistic organizations in my community, both in and outside the performing arts, that I could partner with? (When creative people get together, there is often a flow of new ideas. When two art forms create works in concert around a particular subject or theme, there are expanded opportunities for co-promotion and richer artistic creation. So go out and find an artist or administrator from another cultural institution in your town, get together, and toss around some ideas.)
- Should I be giving my product away for free? (Especially if you are running a small or recently founded organization, giving your product—e.g., your performances, perhaps your recorded music, or your educational resources—away for free might be the right move. Weigh the potential revenue from ticket sales or fees against the level of exposure and attendance that free events are likely to generate. Perhaps a combination of free events and paid, ticketed events might make sense. Perhaps you should give away your educational resources but charge for performances, or vice versa. We are certainly not advocating that free is always the best choice, but as Sir Clive Gillinson points out, for some organizations it is the optimal way to get others motivated about your mission, and it can help put you in a good position to raise funds.)

- Are there communities in my town or city that don't traditionally have access to the performing arts? Can I strengthen my own organization and benefit those communities by finding a way to engage them?

Tips

- Before you sign on at an organization, determine if it has a strong sense of identity coupled with a strong sense of mission. In other words, do the people there know who they are and what they are trying to achieve in the world? If the answer is yes, your future bosses and coworkers will likely be much happier and more productive people than if your answer is no. If you are running your own organization, take a step back and evaluate whether you have a clear sense of your mission and identity. It can make all the difference in the quality of your day-to-day working life.

- It never pays to be inauthentic, especially if the reason is to avoid saying what you think others might not want to hear. We're not saying you should go out of your way to be blunt or to hurt others' feelings, or that you always need to say what's on your mind. But when it comes down to the important moments in your career, respectfully staying true to your inner convictions and your conclusions about any given situation will benefit you in the long run. You'll be doing your colleagues a favor because they will know you better and know where you stand. You'll be doing yourself a favor because you'll avoid situations that become painful or undesirable down the road. And don't just respond to external circumstances authentically. Create your own projects that come from the deepest, truest part of yourself. You may not always succeed, but finding the motivation and clarity of purpose to do the work won't be difficult, and that's more than half the battle.

Exercises

- Pick somebody in a performing arts organization in your community who does what you want to do, and ask her for an informational interview. When you meet with her, ask her about the guiding principles that have been most important in shaping her career. Talk to her about how she got her current job and about previous stages of her career. If you're shy about doing this, imagine yourself in her shoes. Ask yourself: Would you mind if an ambitious young performer came to ask for advice? You'd probably be flattered and ready to help.

- Plot your current activities on the Opportunity Framework. Is there anything that's a drag on both mission fulfillment and resources? Is there anything that's right in the sweet spot of mission fulfillment and sustainability? Are there opportunities you can seek out and create to balance out your Framework?

- Tag yourself. A good tagline, like the one for American Ballet Theatre ("Bringing dance to America and American dance to the world"), can stick in the minds of potential audience members as well as give you or your organization a clearer sense of mission. To come up with a tagline, try describing yourself or your organization in just a few words. Don't overthink it. The clearer and more concise, the better. Just try to sum up what you do and what you offer to the world. And don't worry about getting it right the first time. Advertisers are paid handsomely to come up with taglines for commercial businesses. So try writing a lot of potential versions—10, 20, 30. Keep plugging away and one will stand out. If you're in an ensemble or working in an organization, invite everybody to join in. You never know where the next bright idea might come from. As with all the exercises in this book, you're at your most creative if you're having fun.

ESSENTIAL LESSONS FROM THE ARTIST-ENTREPRENEURS

In this chapter, we present profiles of five artist-entrepreneurs.

1. Claire Chase, artistic director and CEO, the International Contemporary Ensemble
2. Daniel Talbott, artistic director and founder, Rising Phoenix Repertory
3. Christopher Dylan Herbert, baritone, New York Polyphony
4. Loni Landon and Gregory Dolbashian, cofounders, The Playground
5. Alex Lipowski, cofounder and executive director, the Talea Ensemble

These are early- to mid-career, classically trained performing artists who have found ways to make a profession out of their art form while operating outside of existing institutions and traditional career paths. In each case, these artist-entrepreneurs have had to develop business and managerial skills to do so. By telling their stories, we aim to pass on some of those skills to you.

Like the managers profiled in Chapter 6, these five individuals have been recognized by their peers as leaders and innovators. Unlike the managers, everybody profiled here has also been recognized as a first-class performing artist. We think they are an amazing bunch and are happy to introduce them to you.

In addition to offering you some useful concepts, this chapter will also give you snapshots of life after graduation. There are some difficult moments in these stories, when these young artists had to stare down poverty, self-doubt, and judgment from their elders. If it sometimes seems like your life in the arts is coming to pieces around you, rest assured that you're in good company. At some points, every successful career seems as if it is not working. And sometimes, of course, it seems as if everything is coming together perfectly. So we have recorded a few of those triumphant moments, too.

The concepts we explore here are just a handful out of the many that could be extrapolated from each story. We couldn't possibly include everything that could be learned from each of our artist-entrepreneurs, or this book would have no end. And we realize too that there is some conceptual overlap in the qualities we've chosen, both here and in the profiles in Chapter 6. The set of skills necessary to find the right branding for your organization (see Rachel S. Moore's story in Chapter 6) are in some ways similar to the ones it takes to find your niche and fill it (see Loni Landon and Gregory Dolbashian's story in this chapter). The study of leadership and management is not an exact science. In each profile, we've picked out just one salient quality. While a book like this has to explain one concept at a time, a living, breathing artist-entrepreneur displays mastery of many of these concepts simultaneously.

To get the most from this chapter, you don't have to read it straight through. You can pick and choose whichever sections seem most relevant to your career right now. Like success in the arts, there is no one right path.

CLAIRE CHASE, ARTISTIC DIRECTOR AND CEO, THE INTERNATIONAL CONTEMPORARY ENSEMBLE

AVOIDING MISSION CREEP

In military strategy, "mission creep" happens when the major objectives of a campaign are slowly but surely crowded out by the other problems that arise in the course of fighting a war. Mission creep is dangerous because it is invisible to its victims. Each specific diversion can have a good reason behind it. It is true that troops need to be fed and clothed, rivers need to be bridged, and supply chains need to be kept intact, but solving each of those smaller problems may still not add up to winning the war. A good commander needs to combine tactical skill, which is the ability to solve small problems, and strategic vision, which is the ability to keep your eyes on the bigger prize. Sometimes, in order to win the war, you have to sacrifice or ignore smaller wins, or take risks that seem foolish until you see how they fit into the larger plan. Sometimes, you even have to pass up opportunities to defend progress already hard won.

Mission creep is also a danger in management. When an arts not-for-profit has struggled long and hard just to achieve reliable solvency, for example, maintaining that solvency can come to seem more important than actually making art. Day by day, month by month, just keeping your organization afloat can slowly erode your ability to see and commit to your larger purpose.

Claire Chase—founder, artistic director, and CEO of the International Contemporary Ensemble (ICE)—has both tactical skill and strategic vision. At key points in her career and in the development of ICE, she has taken risks or passed up smaller gains in order to move one step closer to achieving her bigger ambitions. As Chase puts it, she has cultivated a habit of "turning success back into risk."[1] Unlike the aims in the military analogy above, Chase's aims are peaceful, but her career is an excellent example of avoiding mission creep and how staying committed to your vision over the long haul pays off.

STRATEGIC VISION

In 2001, Chase graduated from Oberlin with a degree in music and was on a long bus ride to her future home city of Chicago. On the bus, she had a vision of forming a new ensemble devoted to performing contemporary music. From the start, Chase imagined her new ensemble impacting not just a single city but someday fostering radical experimentation in multiple cities across the American classical music landscape.[2]

Part of Chase's inspiration in that moment, which would eventually lead to her creation of ICE, was a European contemporary classical music group called Ensemble Modern, founded in 1980 and based in Frankfurt, Germany. Chase wanted ICE to emulate Ensemble Modern's unconventional management structure, where there is no maestro running the show but where all decisions, including repertoire choice, are made democratically. She also wanted ICE to have Ensemble Modern's prestige and rate of output, which in 2001 (the year of Chase's fateful bus ride) was more than 100 concerts per year, some at Europe's top venues.[3]

After Chase got off the bus in Chicago, she wasted no time making her vision a reality. Her very first action was to have a friend swipe her into a Northwestern University computer lab so she could start sending emails and looking up information about how to get grants and start a not-for-profit. Even though she was starting from scratch, Chase took calculated risks and dreamed big: "Rather than having a concert series where we would try and sell tickets and get people to come to a few concerts a season, I thought, 'No, we need to do a festival. We need to make it everywhere.'"[4] Charged by her vision, Chase made rapid progress. Just three years into its existence, ICE had picked up numerous mentions in the Chicago press and was putting on shows at ten different Chicago venues, each show premiering a new work by an emerging local composer.

In those early years, Chase ran ICE out of her living room and didn't pay herself a cent. She worked catering jobs to make ends meet, playing various employers off one another to get the best hourly wage so she could maximize her time creating new music and planning concerts. While some might succumb to the strain of such a life, Chase had two priceless assets that protected her: vision and grit. Her musical education, which had demanded countless hours of dedicated practice, had taught Chase persistence in the service of higher goals. And her ability to hold her higher vision firmly in mind, despite the daily smaller challenges, kept her on the right path.

TACTICAL CHALLENGES

The challenges of those early years were not just musical but financial. During ICE's first year, Chase applied for 13 grants and was rejected 13 times. During the second year, she upped the number of grant applications to 15 and was rejected for all of those, too. It wasn't until ICE's third year that Chase got some traction, succeeding with one grant application out of 17.[5]

After such a hardscrabble start, you can imagine Chase scaling back her vision for ICE or growing more cautious in her use of whatever funds became available. It was crucial to ICE's later success that Chase did not succumb to either of those tendencies, however reasonable it might have seemed to do so.

In 2010, nine years after ICE was founded, Chase faced down her biggest tactical challenge yet. It didn't come in the form of a problem but a blessing. The Andrew W. Mellon Foundation, among the world's largest grant-making organizations focused on the arts and humanities, invited ICE to apply for a grant in its Arts and Cultural Heritage program area. While an invitation to apply was no guarantee of future funding, it did mean that there was a high likelihood that ICE's application would succeed. The Mellon Foundation is a $6 billion philanthropic enterprise, and its grants can transform organizations like ICE.

In 2010, ICE was doing well. It had grown into a two-city organization performing a dozen or so concerts per year. Two parts of Chase's initial vision had been realized: an unconventional management structure and a pure dedication to the creation and performance of contemporary classical music. But ICE still fell short of Chase's vision for a higher concert output and national cultural visibility.

In applying for the Mellon grant, Chase had a choice. She could apply for nonspecific funding that could be used to cover operational expenses, putting a safety net under ICE as it existed (and remember that it represented almost a decade of Chase's life's work). Or she could apply for a grant to support an experimental project that would, if successful, propel ICE toward her big vision faster, while forgoing any safety net.

Speaking of the state of ICE in 2010, Chase said, "In many ways we were leveling off and becoming another midsized arts organization. And I saw the potential—we never got there—but I very clearly saw the potential of just hiring more staff, doing more events, paying people more, all of those things that would define success, but I realized that if we went that route, and if we turned this tremendous innovation and momentum into something that already exists, we would be missing an opportunity."[6]

ICELAB

Despite the lure of a safety net, which would have been a huge potential tactical win for ICE as it already existed, Chase chose the riskier path. She applied to Mellon to fund ICElab, an experimental program entirely devoted to accelerating ICE's artistic growth.

ICElab was imagined as a four-year project. Each year, six previously unknown contemporary composers were to be commissioned to produce six original, evening-length works to be performed by ICE. The composers and the musicians would work closely together in extended "incubation residencies," during which the works would be shaped collaboratively. The traditional commissioning model in which the composer dreams up the music in isolation from the musicians was to be discarded. Furthermore, the definition of "composer" was expanded to include "anyone working in a creative discipline that involves sound." Everything ICElab produced was to be extensively documented on the Web. ICElab also continued ICE's "normal" practice of having the musicians themselves rotate in and out of and collaborate on all tasks traditionally reserved for full-time administrators. Not a penny of the grant was to be spent on operational support. Everything about ICElab was new or a continuation of something unconventional that ICE was already doing.

If it succeeded, ICElab had the potential to take Chase and ICE to new heights of success and prominence, in line with Chase's initial vision. If it fizzled, ICE would find itself no safer financially than it was before the prospect of the Mellon grant.

In 2010, Mellon approved a four-year, $340,000 grant to ICE to support ICElab. Chase was thrilled at the chance to use more resources than she'd ever dreamed of to keep her organization as energetic and edgy as it was when it was first founded.[7] ICElab's first season was in 2011. By the completion of its final season in 2015, it achieved all its stated goals, premiering 24 works by 25 emerging composers over four years.[8]

The increased visibility caused by ICElab's furious output has paid off, and there are signs that ICE is becoming the fixture in the American classical music establishment that Chase hoped it would be. The year 2012 marked the first time ICE was asked to perform at the venerable Mostly Mozart Festival, which has been held at Lincoln Center since 1966. Participation in Mostly Mozart is usually reserved for traditional organizations like symphony orchestras and classical chamber music ensembles from cities around the United States.

In 2012 and 2013, ICE released its first two albums under its own record label, with the decidedly cool name TUNDRA. Both albums were written up in the *New York Times*, which has given no fewer than six favorable mentions to ICElab concerts.

Most tellingly, Chase was chosen by the MacArthur Foundation for a "genius" grant in 2012. Called an "arts entrepreneur" by MacArthur, she was honored as much for her skills as a trailblazing innovator in arts management as she was for her talents as a musician. In addition to the huge cultural prestige a MacArthur genius award brings (recent recipients have included Junot Diaz, a Pulitzer Prize–winning novelist; Jad Abumrad, host of NPR's *Radiolab*; and jazz saxophonist Steve Coleman, hailed by his generation as the successor to John Coltrane), the $500,000 award has made a great deal more possible for both Chase and ICE itself.

Had she chosen the tactically safer path in 2010, ICE would no doubt still be a healthy organization, but it would not have grown so quickly and so visibly toward Chase's bold vision. Of ICElab, Chase said, "The results are fantastic; we're having a blast. We're creating more new material than we ever have in the past, and at a faster pace. We're learning more, and we're growing—at the speed of light."[9]

★ ★ ACHIEVING YOUR VISION ★ ★

In telling Claire Chase's story, we talk about the difference between enacting a long-term, strategic plan and solving smaller, tactical problems along the way. Another way to think about this concept is by differentiating between visions and goals:

- Your **vision** for the future of your organization or individual career is the big picture. It is where you see yourself in five or ten years or beyond. It is the stuff of your wildest, biggest dreams.
- Your **goals** are the smaller, intermediate steps you need to take to get you to your vision.

It might seem like an obvious thing to say, but having a clear vision and a set of goals to achieve it is crucial to success, especially in the flexible and sometimes freewheeling performing arts world, where it can be easy to get distracted. As Henry David Thoreau said, "In the long run, men hit only what they aim at. Therefore, though they should fail immediately, they had better aim at something high."

Diane Wittry, conductor of the Allentown Symphony Orchestra, recommends planning your career in reverse. Start out looking at the future with a clear vision of where you want to be, and then connect it back up, via intermediate goals, to where you are now. Try to imagine how long it will take you to accomplish each goal, and incorporate that into your planning. At every stage in your career, says Wittry, you'll be at a point where you'll have to choose between a number of options. Remembering the path back from your ultimate vision will help you discern the right choice to make. While your goals are almost certainly going to change over the course of your career, as long as your vision is strong, you'll be able to stay on track. The most important quality a vision can have, says Wittry, is specificity. In her case, she didn't just know she wanted to be a conductor—she knew she wanted to be the conductor of a regional, midsize orchestra like the one in Allentown, Pennsylvania. The more specific your vision, the easier it will be to plot a course straight to it.[10]

Don't forget to include your future finances when plotting out your vision and goals. Include your future yearly earnings or the eventual budget for your now fledgling organization. When it comes to money, take a page from your artistic career and dream big. Be as specific as possible:

How many new works or gigs would you like to perform in a given year? How many full-time dancers or musicians do you want to have on your payroll? Questions like these will fine-tune your goals and let you pace your progress so you don't get bogged down or lost on your journey.

None of this should make you afraid of experimenting and taking risks, even concerning which goals and visions you incorporate into your career plan to begin with. You don't have to get it right the first time to get real-world traction with your vision and goals. It is far better to have a plan that you change a hundred times than to have no plan at all.

If you're not sure what your vision is, then chances are you need to get out in the real world and experiment with what you enjoy and what you are good at. Planning is crucial, but without the insights that come from direct experience, it won't be enough to move your career forward. So don't be afraid to get out there and try new things, fail, succeed, and above all learn. As the ancient Roman proverb says: "Fortune helps those who are daring."

DANIEL TALBOTT, ARTISTIC DIRECTOR AND FOUNDER, RISING PHOENIX REPERTORY

ADAPTABILITY

In Chapter 1, we advised you to be willing to walk an indirect career path, and in this chapter, we extol the importance of devoting yourself to a single vision. Those might seem like two contradictory pieces of advice, but we prefer to think of them as coexisting ideals that require constant rebalancing. At some points in your career, single-minded effort will work best, while at others, a flexible, open-minded approach will move you forward. As the great psychologist Havelock Ellis said, "All the art of living lies in a fine mingling of letting go and holding on." One word for the capacity to alternate holding on and letting go is *adaptability*, and a fine example of it is the actor, director, producer, playwright, and literary manager Daniel Talbott.

Talbott is the artistic director and founder of Rising Phoenix Repertory. He graduated from Juilliard in 2002 with a degree in drama, and he founded Rising Phoenix Rep while he was still an undergraduate. He splits his time between Brooklyn and Los Angeles and works on productions for Rising Phoenix Rep and other companies in both places. Talbott's work includes film and TV roles, but his guiding passion has always been live theater. He has produced, directed, or written dozens of plays, and he's won numerous awards, including a Theater Hall of Fame Fellowship, a New York Innovative Theatre Award, a Drama-Logue Award, and a Lucille Lortel Award for producing. He is supported entirely by income from his acting, directing, producing, and playwriting work.[11]

We chose Talbott to profile for this book because he is a successful actor, director, and playwright who has deliberately pursued a career in the fine arts area of his profession. There is absolutely nothing wrong with wanting to be a big star in film, on TV, or on Broadway. But our primary goal in this book is to aid those whose first aim is to make the art that matters to them, and then build an economic framework to support that process. And while the lessons distilled from Talbott's career are especially relevant to actors, they are valuable for all types of performers.

FROM HOME BASE TO JUILLIARD

Before Talbott discovered theater, he was sure his life was headed in another direction: baseball. In the midst of a tumultuous childhood, baseball had been Talbott's haven of stability and structure, and his family expected that his skill and dedication to the sport would carry him through college on a baseball scholarship.

Then Talbott started dating a young woman who was part of the Young Conservatory Program at the American Conservatory Theater (A.C.T.) in San Francisco. She and Talbott acted in amateur sci-fi and horror films together, and she eventually introduced him to acting for the stage. The relationship didn't pan out for Talbott, but theater did. During his first moments in the Young Conservatory Program, Talbott, speaking over the phone from Los Angeles in the hours before a Rising Phoenix Rep rehearsal, said he had a kind of conversion experience: "Theater was like finding the girl you want to marry and die with. I didn't know if I was good at it. I had never done it. I had barely seen any plays. But for whatever reason, walking into that building that day on 30 Grant Avenue in San Francisco I just, for the first time in my life—and I know it sounds a little spiritual and crazy—but, for the first time in my life, I was like, 'I'm gonna do this.'"[12]

Talbott's entire life did indeed take a new direction starting at that moment. But just having a new vision was not enough to propel him into a career pursuing it. He would have to adapt to new ways of supporting himself and of thinking about his work. The effects of pursuing a new long-term goal in one's career, even a positive and inspiring one, can be disruptive.

Talbott's grandparents, with whom he was living when he discovered theater, were dismayed by his abandonment of baseball and withdrew their financial support. Talbott was then only a junior in high school. He adapted by undergoing the arduous legal process necessary to become an emancipated minor, which allowed him to start legally living on his own before the age of 18. He moved out of his grandparents' house and to Oakland, California, where he started working as an actor as soon as possible. While he had to work so he could eat and pay the bills, Talbott's early theatrical education was subsidized by a full scholarship to the Young Conservatory Program. He says that the hardship of leaving home proved to be a great blessing because it showed him what he really wanted. Any ambition other than acting, he says, would not have motivated him to work and pay for his new life entirely on his own.

Within two years of leaving home, Talbott was cobbling together a living from his art, combining stage, film, and television work into a sustainable life, albeit barely sustainable at first.

Shifting from baseball to acting also required that Talbott adapt himself to new ways of thinking and new methods of acquiring skills. At first, he approached acting with the same athletic overintensity of his baseball training. This produced stiff, clunky performances. Talbott admits that he wasn't a very good actor during his first two years. It wasn't until he embraced an ease and openness in his approach that he began to see positive results.

Most fateful of all, Talbott allowed himself to adapt to the idea, however briefly, that he might be good enough to get into Juilliard. It was Amy Potozkin, associate artistic and head casting director at the Bay Area–based Berkeley Repertory Theatre, who pushed Talbott to audition for Juilliard. He was absolutely convinced that he wasn't good enough get in. Talbott found Juilliard's reputation intimidating rather than enticing. Moreover, he couldn't even afford the $100 audition fee. But Potozkin covered the fee and was firm in her encouragement. Talbott surrendered to the audition process and gave it his all, setting aside prior ideas about the limits of what he could achieve. Staying open-minded for the hour or so it took to complete the audition paid off handsomely. Not only did Talbott get in but he got a full scholarship.

Juilliard would transform Talbott's life and build the foundations for his future career. The network of fellow performing artists that would initially constitute Rising Phoenix Rep were all Juilliard connections, and enmeshing himself in the Juilliard community firmly established Talbott in New York City, the center of the American theatrical scene. Had he not allowed himself to entertain the idea, however tenuously and briefly, that he might be good enough to gain admission, Talbott's future career would never have been launched.

DETOUR DAYS

Talbott had known since before Juilliard that he wanted a company of his own, where he and his closest colleagues could find steady work and artistic freedom. After waiting one year to get settled into the pace of life at Juilliard and in New York City, Talbott founded Rising Phoenix Rep while still a sophomore. During the summers, he set about producing and directing professional work, even though Juilliard has its drama students sign a contract saying they will not take on professional acting work before graduation. Once again displaying an ability to adapt his artistic ambitions to any situation, Talbott pointed out that the contract prohibited only acting, not writing, producing, or directing. Juilliard responded to Talbott's audacity with support and lent him space to develop his fledgling company. The work he started with Rising Phoenix Rep as an undergraduate has continued unbroken ever since.

From the start, Talbott wanted Rising Phoenix Rep to be a place where actors, playwrights, and directors would have total artistic freedom. He also wanted it to be a base from which he and others could venture out and take on work in film, TV, and other live theater, while always having an artistic home to return to. It wasn't until a major crisis that Talbott was to discover how best to make this model work.

In the early 2000s, Talbott and company tried to mount a production of *Fen* by the English playwright Caryl Churchill. It was an ambitious undertaking for a small company like Rising Phoenix Rep. After securing the rights to the play, the company rented Walkerspace at the Soho Rep in Manhattan, and raised $60,000, which would have made the production officially "Off-Broadway" according to the rules of the Actors' Equity Association (AEA), the union for stage actors. Rising Phoenix Rep had hitherto produced only Off-Off-Broadway shows, which AEA defines as having a budget of $35,000 or less. But for this show, Talbott and company had upped their game, hoping *Fen* would help them down the path to becoming an established Off-Broadway company with their own permanent space and staff, like New York Theatre Workshop, Second Stage, or Playwrights Horizons.[13]

Just five days before the curtain for *Fen* was to go up, disaster struck in the form of stratospheric, unmissable opportunities for two of the cast members, who were also Talbott's friends. One got a role in a major feature film and another got a role in a major TV show, both offering salaries that soared above the small (though honorable) compensation that Rising Phoenix Rep was offering for being in *Fen*.

Preventing the two cast members from following their good fortune went against the spirit of Rising Phoenix Rep, but so did canceling the show, since it would break that sacred law of theater: "The show must go on." Talbott and company had to find a way to let their colleagues go but also preserve the honor of the company.

So just five days before opening night, with a city full of advertisements for *Fen*, a theater full of nearly completed sets, and a substantial, nonrefundable investment in renting Walkerspace, Talbott and company found themselves without a play. Actors have a reputation for being superstitious, and Talbott is no exception. "I think the theater gods are tricksters," he says. "They like to mess with you to see how you're going to respond. They love jokes and they love comedy. So watching you fall on your face is funny to them. Looking at it this way helps you see the possibility in failure, and the chance to dig deeper than before and see how you can flip something negative into something positive."[14]

As he had earlier in life, Talbott held on to his vision and found a new way to realize it by adapting to the circumstances. He drew on his extensive contacts within the richly populated New York theater scene and brainstormed with the rest of the company about what they could achieve in just five days.

The result was *Detour Days*, a multiday festival of ten or so ambitious projects, including two Tennessee Williams one-acts directed by celebrated Off-Broadway director Trip Cullman; *The Liddy Plays* by fellow Juilliard grad, novelist, and playwright Brooke Berman; and a production of *Blue Remembered Hills* by Dennis Potter, helmed by another noted Off-Broadway director, Michael Sexton. There were also workshops and two plays that were conceived, written, directed, and performed entirely within 24 hours. The sets for *Fen* were abandoned or repurposed, and anything else the group needed was begged, borrowed, or stolen. They took a couch from a friend's apartment, scavenged a bunch of chairs from the garbage, and scoured antique shops for props. When they needed a bed, Talbott chipped in his own. They paid a techie from Juilliard in pizza and beer to hang the lights. To promote the impromptu festival, they went to all the marketing outlets they had engaged to promote *Fen* and put a positive spin on their predicament, proclaiming that they had decided to go in a bold new direction with *Detour Days*.

After the smoke cleared, Talbott and company discovered that they had produced something more diverse, daring, and ambitious than what they had originally planned. The experience even gave Talbott an enduring new vision for the future of his company: "With *Detour Days*, it was so much more alive and fun, and so much more work got supported and done than just that one play. It taught us to be agile."[15] Talbott discovered that Rising Phoenix Rep didn't need to work big to achieve big artistic ambitions. In fact, the entire budget for *Detour Days* ended up barely breaking the $4,000 mark. This was not only less than the $60,000 raised to produce *Fen* but well below the $35,000 cap that the AEA puts on Equity Showcases, or Off-Off-Broadway productions.

Off-Off-Broadway productions (that's two *offs*) differ from Off-Broadway (that's just one *off*) productions in both budget and administrative requirements. Both can take place only in theaters with no more than 99 seats (though, in practice, Off-Off-Broadway shows often take place in much smaller venues, like the back rooms of bars, repurposed industrial spaces, or even homes). Shows produced for more than $35,000 get kicked up into the Off-Broadway bracket, and the amount of paperwork and the number of rules you have to follow also increases. Off-Off-Broadway shows allow professional, unionized actors to mount small productions that put them on display to producers, directors, and their peers, while still respecting union rules. They also allow pro actors to experiment or just have fun while still working at a professional level. It's important to remember that there is no negative connotation about the word *off* in this context. In the professional theater world, it is just used to denote what level of resources are gathered for a particular production and what rules have to be followed.[16]

Without the frantic schedule of *Detour Days*, Talbott and company might never have realized the full range of artistic possibilities achievable with the Off-Off-Broadway model. What had started as a crisis and potential failure ended up, through heroic efforts, as a breakthrough. Talbott realized that he never wanted to leave the Off-Off-Broadway mode of production fully behind. So rather than keep Rising Phoenix Rep on track to become an Off-Broadway company with its own theater and staff, Talbott chose to keep his company small, able to pivot quickly between producing either Off-Broadway or Off-Off-Broadway, depending on the ambition of each project and how much time and money were available. Once you have built your own permanent Off-Broadway production apparatus, you can't go back, says Talbott. You have to keep feeding the machine you've built, and vital artistic freedom gets lost. You can no longer, to use Talbott's example, decide on a whim to do a production of *Twelfth Night* by Shakespeare in the back room of a tavern for one night on a budget of $5. You would have your full-time production staff tapping their feet, without a job to do and no money to pay them with anyway. Talbott's example is not a glib one. Freewheeling companies of talented performers have kept the performing arts vital since the Middle Ages, and experimental, small productions are deeply meaningful artistic experiences for Talbott, his colleagues, and their audiences.

Talbott respects and loves the established Off-Broadway companies, and he believes that the American theater landscape would be lost without them. He and his wife, Addie—a fellow actor who also sits on Rising Phoenix Rep's board—have both worked for the well-respected Off-Broadway indie theater incubator New York Theatre Workshop, and Talbott says Rising Phoenix Rep could not have taken shape without the Workshop's guidance and support. But for Rising Phoenix Rep, staying small and adaptable has been the best way to achieve artistic success.

By engaging production partners rather than building its own permanent Off-Broadway apparatus, Rising Phoenix Rep has the freedom to produce plays with a budget of $5 in one month and a budget of $800,000 the next. About half of the shows Rising Phoenix Rep produces each year are in the Off-Broadway bracket, while the other half are Off-Off-Broadway. It is a business model capable of adapting to whatever amount of time, artists, and financing is available, and it has allowed Talbott and Rising Phoenix Rep to work more or less constantly.

When he produces at the Off-Broadway level, Talbott partners with Rattlestick Playwrights Theater, where he is one of the literary managers. Rising Phoenix Rep often makes use of Rattlestick's dedicated performance space in New York's Greenwich Village and the spaces Rattlestick uses in Los Angeles. Rising Phoenix Rep also partners with Snug Harbor Productions, WeatherVane Productions, and piece by piece productions. These coproducing partners have a permanent capacity to handle the financing and contractual apparatus demanded by the AEA for all productions over $35,000, as well as deal with the general management challenges that inevitably crop up in bigger productions.

"YOU CAN ALWAYS BE WORKING"

Like just about every aspect of his life, Talbott structured Rising Phoenix Rep's business model to be of maximum service to his theatrical work and to make it possible for him to create work in collaboration with other artists, given any amount of available time and money. If he had two weeks, $20, and a bathtub, Talbott jokes, he'd find a writer, commission a play, and find other actors willing to sign on. His desire to work no matter what has driven him to become an artist-entrepreneur, though he wouldn't phrase it that way. To him, he's just trying to stay in the game as an artist. "You are an artist because of the work that you do. You are an artist because you create art. You can always be working," he says.[17]

Rising Phoenix Repertory's name is well suited to the dramatic reversals in its founder's life at the time of his conversion to theater. And it is equally suited to the revival of the company's fortunes after the near disaster of *Detour Days*. But Talbott says he took the name from the nature of theater itself. A live performance burns brightly while it is still going on, but it is extinguished when the performance ends. Yet every time actors and audiences gather again, the show is resurrected and goes on.

CHRISTOPHER DYLAN HERBERT, BARITONE, NEW YORK POLYPHONY

STRIKING A BALANCE IN SMALL ENSEMBLES

New York Polyphony's artistic mantra is "balance, not blend," which refers to the unique sound that has earned the four-man vocal ensemble two Grammy nominations, a fully booked touring and concert schedule, and high praise from the music press in the United States and Europe. Because New York Polyphony (NYP) has only four voices, one to a vocal part, each member has to trust the other three to hit their notes more or less perfectly every time they sing. Every performance is an exacting exercise in precision and mutual trust. "Balance, not blend" is also an encapsulation of NYP's business philosophy. While they have professional talent representation, the four singers divide all the group's remaining management activities among themselves. While big decisions are made collectively, each member independently carries out an ongoing and distinct set of duties essential to the group's regular operation. As with their music, there is no larger membership to pick up the slack, and it has taken years of disciplined work to build up to the full capacity at which they now operate. Their balanced self-management style is a great model for any small group of performers.

In an interview at a café near the Brooklyn Academy of Music, Chris Herbert, NYP's baritone and the group's de facto business manager, explains how in just two years the group went from having strong musical capacity but uneven business practices to maximizing its potential in both areas.

When Herbert joined NYP in 2010, the group was giving just 10 to 12 concerts per year. As of 2014, NYP was holding steady at about 50 concerts per year, a mark it hit in 2012. That is enough to provide a solid, predictable income for the members (a rare thing in the freelance performing arts world), and it's limited only by the amount of time the group wants to spend on the road. "Right now," says Herbert, "we are at the limit of how much we can tour."[18]

Going from scraping together just a few concerts to choosing at will how many the group performs was a multistep process. And it began, says Herbert, with a single sheet of paper.

BALANCING THE DISTRIBUTION OF RESPONSIBILITY

Though Herbert was tapped by NYP for his baritone voice, he also brought business skills to the table, which he learned from the board members of Sing for Hope, an arts-focused nonprofit he worked for during the 2000s. Chief among those skills, says Herbert, is the ability to set clearly defined goals that you can measure your progress toward. But before you can measure progress, he says, you have to know where you are to begin with. This was knowledge NYP didn't have in 2010, either in its finances or its management structure.

Herbert's first business question to Craig Phillips, NYP's bass and one of its hardworking cofounders, was "Who does what?" Phillips wasn't entirely sure, and neither were the group's two other members. So Herbert got out a sheet of blank paper, divided it into four equal quadrants, and wrote a group member's name at the top of each. Then each member said in turn what he did, in addition to his musical responsibilities, and Herbert wrote that info under the name. The resulting piece of paper was visually unbalanced. The boxes for Phillips and Geoffrey Williams, NYP's countertenor and other cofounder, were full of duties, while the other two members' boxes were mostly empty. Says Herbert, "It was amazing to see just how much two of the guys were doing and how little me and the other member were doing. That visualization helped everybody."[19] Worse, there was duplication and ambiguity in the existing distribution, which meant that certain key tasks were being delayed or dropped.

The first part of the solution was to balance out the sheet visually. The group redistributed responsibilities evenly among the four members, with some consideration for skill and preference. Herbert took on travel and finances, which he still manages. The duties that fell to the other members during that meeting still remain with them, too.

The second part of the solution was to take any floating tasks and assign them to just one member. The resulting balanced management structure was a relief for everybody. It lifted the drag on productivity caused by lingering resentment over (1) the sense that not everyone was pulling his weight and (2) the annoyance and inefficiency caused by the endless shuffling around of vaguely assigned tasks.

BALANCING THE BOOKS

Like balancing the distribution of responsibility, balancing the books started with information gathering. When Herbert took his first look into NYP's business checkbook, he was initially pleased. He saw a page with a perforated edge where checks had been written and torn out. To the left of the place where each check had been was a record of the date, the payee, and the amount. Then Herbert turned the page. The checks there were also torn out, but the information about them was missing. The records had all been left blank. As he flipped through the checkbook, Herbert saw that four years' worth of checks had been written and torn out with no record having been made. When he turned to the group's bank to reconstruct the records, Herbert was stymied by an unhelpful bureaucracy. It was only the photographic memory of Williams, who remembered what checks had been written despite not having been in charge of the group's money, that allowed Herbert to reconstruct NYP's past finances. Even though it was painstaking work, Herbert felt it was worth it, because without past records it would be impossible to set future financial goals. Once again, you cannot move toward where you want to be if you don't know where you are and where you've been.

Gaining clarity about the group's financial situation swept away a negative attitude toward money in NYP that is understandably common among artists. Because they don't often make much money, artists can avoid looking closely at their finances, which naturally makes it impossible to run a business well. With a balanced checkbook, NYP's members were not afraid to know just how much money they made.

This allowed them to set clear financial goals for the first time. Any lingering sense of unease about money was replaced by a newfound motivation and even a sense of adventure about what they could achieve.

Herbert also instituted a yearly budgeting process that, instead of being a chore, actually served to knit the group more closely together. Before having a balanced checkbook and clearly defined areas of responsibility, the members had spent their own money on business expenses, often with uncertain hope of reimbursement. If Williams, the group's de facto musical director, had wanted to take a composer out to lunch, he had to pay for it himself. It was the same if Steven Caldicott Wilson, the group's tenor, had wanted to purchase new ties for a photo shoot.

Herbert had a two-pronged reform for expenses. First, he got a shared credit card that members could use to pay for group expenses, at their own discretion. Being simultaneously entrusted to spend the group's money and also assured that it wouldn't come out of their own pockets boosted everybody's morale, says Herbert. It also made everybody more willing to spend whatever was needed to get their jobs done. The second part of the solution was to ask each member at a start-of-year budget meeting how much money he needed allocated to his area of responsibility. This was another spot where past record keeping made future financial health easier to manage. By knowing exactly how much had been spent on his areas in the past, each member could be confident of his estimates for the future. Having his own sub-budget also gave each member an increased sense of ownership and a bigger psychological buy-in to NYP's collective financial welfare.

Two additional changes to the group's cash flow had the same effect. Herbert started what he called the "one-fifth" policy. When profits came in from a concert, management fees and expenses were deducted from them, and the remainder was to be split five rather than four ways. One-fifth went to each of the four singers, but the remaining fifth went into a company bank account, used to pay off the shared credit card. By making this an automatic part of the budgeting process, the members no longer had to worry about cash flow. The one-fifth policy turned New York Polyphony itself into a fifth group member, which served and continues to serve as a reminder of the group's collective welfare.

To further increase a sense of autonomy and buy-in when it came to their individual sub-budgets, Herbert also instituted an end-of-the-year bonus, to be drawn from the one-fifth account and distributed evenly once a year. The bonus provides continuous motivation to each member to keep his expenses as low as reasonably possible.

In part because of the new cash flow process, NYP's budget doubled every year from 2010 to 2013, and it stayed at the same level in 2014.[20] Herbert is quick to point out that he's not the only reason for the group's success. Cofounders Craig Phillips and Geoffrey Williams sweated it out for four years to establish NYP's artistic reputation, setting the stage for the group's current financial success. Herbert says he came along at just the right time to nudge the group in a financially sounder and more ambitious direction. "All the immense growth is not because of me," he says, "but I think we're able to measure it because of me."[21] He also believes that balancing NYP's books has brought its musical artistry to a higher level. Worrying just enough (but not too much) about money to have confidence in the group's financial footing has freed up more mental energy for the members to devote to their music.

BALANCING WORK AND LIFE

Balancing their shared responsibility and their books has led NYP to what, for most performing artists, is a luxury problem: having so much steady work that they need to find sustainable work-life balance. Life in a small ensemble is intimate and intense. Herbert got married to his partner, conductor Timothy Long, in the summer of 2010. He likes to joke, "I married Tim, and then a few months later I joined New York Polyphony and got married to three other men." Finding room for family and time for other musical outlets besides NYP is a necessary challenge for all four members. Even when the members of a small ensemble work as well together as those of NYP, there is a need for ruthless realism about just how much time everybody is capable of spending together. Says Herbert, "Two weeks at a time, maximum. That's how much we can tour. We would kill each other otherwise." On the road, the group has met other small ensembles, including string quartets and other four-part vocal groups, who agree with the two-week touring limit. Knowing when to step away from work is just as important as building up to a maximum capacity for it.[22]

As a performer-manager, it is also crucial to strike a balance in your own mind between business and art. Herbert says he can sometimes get so wrapped up in winning all the various battles of day-to-day management that he forgets why he's in music in the first place and not making a lot more money in another profession. Keeping his higher purpose in mind keeps him focused and content with where he is and what he's doing.

"Sometimes it feels like the most existentially pointless task that we're doing, and I question its value," says Herbert, referring to the group's music in particular and classical music in general. But all it takes is the thrill of a great performance, or meaningful feedback from a fan, and Herbert's zeal for the musical life comes roaring back: "Somebody comes up to you and tells you how much it changed something in them, or how much it meant to them, or what an influence it had. And that makes it all worth it."[23]

LONI LANDON AND GREGORY DOLBASHIAN, COFOUNDERS, THE PLAYGROUND

FINDING YOUR NICHE

At some point in your career, you will have a need that seems impossible to meet. Instead of despairing, consider that you have just come across a golden opportunity. If you have the need, it is likely that others in your profession have it, too. And if you can find a creative way to satisfy your need, you've got an opportunity to make a meaningful contribution to your field, and also a potentially successful business model.

That was the case with Loni Landon and Gregory Dolbashian, two contemporary dancers from New York City who cofounded The Playground, a regular meet-up/happening that provides a place for dancers to rehearse and connect with choreographers and each other. It is difficult to describe The Playground concisely because there has never quite been anything like it in the dance world. It started because Landon and Dolbashian found themselves with a problem: They couldn't afford to dance.

Dancing, both ballet and contemporary, is unlike the other performing arts. Instrumentalists can do the bulk of their rehearsing alone and just about anywhere. The same is true for actors and singers. But dancers need two ingredients that are hard to come by: wide-open spaces and other dancers. Even in places where living spaces aren't as constricted as they are in New York City, it is the rare home that has an empty room the size of a dance studio, not to mention full-length mirrors along the walls. Dancers being able to watch themselves move is equivalent to instrumentalists and singers being able to hear the music they make. There is no point in rehearsing if you can't judge the product.

But just having a studio isn't enough. Being surrounded by other dancers and inspired and challenged by a choreographer are the most essential ingredients of the rehearsal process. Even the most driven and disciplined dancers need others to push them to their full potential.

Gathering all these ingredients together costs money. Professional dance classes in New York City can cost up to $30 per session, and to stay at the top of their game, dancers need to rehearse almost every day.[24] Even at the lowest rates offered by pro dance organizations, five classes a week comes out to $280 per month.[25] That would be expensive even in a profession where the average salary wasn't below the poverty line, as it is for classically trained dancers in New York City.[26] Furthermore, professional classes are one of the few places outside auditions where dancers can catch the eye of a choreographer who might employ them. The ratio of able dancers to available pro jobs in New York is so high, in fact, that most choreographers don't hold auditions at all for fear of being swamped. They just hire dancers they already know.

Add to all these pressures the brutal constraint of time. A dancer doesn't have her entire life to work professionally. Moreover, a dancer's training isn't over until about age 20, and her physical capacity begins to degrade by the age of 35. That leaves a fleeting 15 years in the sun during which a dancer has a chance of breaking through the fierce competition for professional work. For dancers, daily rehearsals at a professional level are a matter of artistic survival.

It was in the crucible of all these constraints that the idea for The Playground took shape. In 2010, Landon and Dolbashian were sitting in a coffee shop trying to figure out how to keep their careers going. Landon had just returned from a five-year stint in Germany, dancing first for Ballet Theater Munich and then Tanz Munich Theater. It is easier to make a living as a dancer in Europe, where government support for the arts keeps jobs plentiful and compensation much higher than in the United States. But once she returned to America, Landon didn't have consistent work, like so many other talented dancers she had met in New York. Dolbashian had just started his own troupe, the DASH ensemble, and felt he was entering the most challenging period of his career so far.

Staring at the table in front of them, she and Dolbashian dreamed of a way to dance that wouldn't cost more per session than the cups of coffee they had just bought. It was the sight of the coffee cups on the table, of their willingness to pay just a little to satisfy a daily need, that triggered The Playground. If a group of dancers came together and chipped in the price of a cup of coffee, Landon and Dolbashian thought, they could afford rehearsal space of their own and maybe have enough left over to pay pro choreographers to lead the sessions.[27]

Their first move was to scout out low-cost studio space for rent at Gibney Dance, a community-oriented dance company with facilities in the heart of Manhattan. The pair then informed the dance community about The Playground via social media and word of mouth. At The Playground's first session, the price point was "donate what you can." Landon and Dolbashian bet on the collective goodwill of the dance community—and lost. After the first session, they had a donation jar filled with granola bars, candy, pennies, and some stray cigarettes. The turnout had been excellent, proving that The Playground was satisfying a real need, but you can't run a business on loose change and cigarettes. Dolbashian and Landon had found their niche, but they didn't quite know how to fill it yet. So they set the price at a flat fee of $5, where it has stayed ever since. The profits from the $5 fee are enough to rent space, pay choreographers, and keep The Playground breaking even.[28]

FILLING YOUR NICHE

If you've found a previously unmet need and come up with a way to satisfy it, don't be afraid to tweak your business model until it is sustainable. Finding your niche isn't the same as knowing how to occupy it over the long term. Be open to experimentation and change in the service of your mission. In fact, to keep your business going over the long haul, you will almost certainly be making small changes all the time.

Playground sessions are two hours long and capped at 30 dancers, to make sure the space doesn't get too crowded and to keep dancers from feeling like they cannot stand out or are unable to connect meaningfully with the choreographer or with each other. Spots are available first come, first served. For the dancers, the benefits are daily rehearsals and face and body time with a professional choreographer. For the roster of The Playground's guest choreographers, the benefits are a small stipend and a large room full of talented dancers who are willing to help them work out new ideas.[29]

From that initial session, Landon and Dolbashian's creation has become a fixture in the New York dance world. They named it The Playground to emphasize its free-form nature—it is neither audition nor formal class—and its friendly, collaborative atmosphere. At a session we attended a few years ago, the vibe was intense, collegial, and wildly experimental. The first hour was devoted to warm-ups, both psychological and physical, and the second hour was spent exploring a piece in process by that day's choreographer and session leader. After the session, the dancers gathered informally in the studio and the hallway outside, brimming with positive energy. Everybody we spoke to was thrilled to be there.

For Dolbashian and Landon, the well-being of the dancers and the dance community is what keeps them going. In an interview on Fordham's campus in October 2013, Landon said, "Once we saw The Playground in action, we said, 'Oh, wow, people are following us and want to support us!' And I think what did it for us was, after a few sessions, that some dancers came up to us and said, 'Thank you so much for doing this.' And at that, I started to cry."[30] When finding your niche means finding a way to be of service to your larger artistic community, it can be an emotionally charged moment in your career. It might feel so good that you'll be hooked.

As of 2015, The Playground is five years old and flourishing. It has received support from the Lower Manhattan Cultural Council, and it was recognized by *Dance Magazine* in 2013 as one of "25 to Watch," a list normally reserved for individual dancers rather than organizations.[31] It has become well known in the New York dance community as an informal job market and gathering place. Landon and Dolbashian have officially partnered with Gina Gibney, choreographer and founder of Gibney Dance, the space where The Playground meets. In addition to providing The Playground with a physical home base at Gibney's space in downtown Manhattan, the partnership has given administrative and developmental support to The Playground and allowed more sessions to be scheduled throughout the year.

ALEX LIPOWSKI, COFOUNDER AND EXECUTIVE DIRECTOR, THE TALEA ENSEMBLE

TENACITY

The root of tenacity is the Latin word *tenere*, which means "to hold." To be tenacious means to hold fast to something. Every performing artist already understands the value of this quality. It is the years spent in practice, holding on to the goal of being a more proficient musician, that turns a novice into a virtuoso. The same holds true for dancers, actors, and all skilled performers.

When applied to the business of the performing arts, holding tenaciously to a single purpose can serve you well. You will no doubt find that in business, more flexibility is required than in your artistic training. Tolerating an inevitable amount of give-and-take will serve you well in negotiations, for example. But holding tenaciously to the big goals of your arts career will ensure that small compromises don't knock you off course.

Alex Lipowski, cofounder of the Talea Ensemble, a contemporary classical group based in New York City, is a great example of tenacity, both in the artistic and business sides of his career. Talea, which he cofounded with composer Anthony Cheung in 2007, moved into permanent headquarters in 2012. The group has worked with some of the greatest names in contemporary classical music, including legendary conductor and composer Pierre Boulez. Lipowski's full-time work is as Talea's executive director, and the group's performances have been well reviewed by the *New York Times* and recommended by *Time Out New York*.[32] This is remarkable, considering the challenging nature of Talea's repertoire, which could be described as unsettling to most people's tastes.

PROFESSOR BAD TRIP

Some of the pieces Talea performs are better described as acoustic environments rather than music with a recognizable melody. Even the sound notation is unconventional. The music for one piece that Lipowski showed us looked more like electrical engineering schematics than musical notes on a traditional staff. Talea's instruments are equally unconventional and can be strangely pleasing yet also grating to the ear. Spring coils from abandoned automobiles and copper bowls scraped along metal plates are just two examples. One piece the group is famous for premiering in the United States is *Professor Bad Trip* by the Italian composer Fausto Romitelli. It is three movements of dissonant sound washes composed of clanky piano notes and melting woodwinds and strings, with sinister electronic undertones. It's like the soundtrack to a nightmare.

What has kept Talea growing since its founding is as much Lipowski's personal devotion to popularizing such music as any virtue of the music itself. Speaking of *Professor Bad Trip* during an interview at Talea's New York City studio, Lipowski said "It embodies the mission of Talea. We don't compromise what we play."[33] An unwillingness to deviate, even from a purpose with such an unlikely prospect of widespread appreciation as contemporary classical music, has characterized Lipowski's entire career.

When he was in high school, his father told him he had to pick a career, telling him that he could choose whatever he wanted. When Lipowski said "I choose music," his father begged him to reconsider. But Lipowski held fast to his passion. Later, at Juilliard, Lipowski chose the kind of challenging contemporary music characterized by *Professor Bad Trip*, and he has never looked back. He says he never had any doubts: "I always knew that new music was the path for me. Not only was music the only way to go but I specifically had to have new music. It's something inside me."[34]

Running Talea has led him to make some compromises. He no longer rehearses as much as he would like to. He says he used to practice for six hours a day and then email for two, but now he emails for six and practices for two. Lipowski has also accepted that there will never be as much government or foundation funding available for contemporary classical in the United States as there is for traditional classical music. But his zealous devotion to the cause of new music has kept him from being discouraged and has helped him develop what he calls a "beautiful relationship" with his patrons.

Says Lipowski: "If we want to have a program, we go to individuals who support and really believe in what we do . . . it's been so inspiring to share in the growth of the ensemble with them—and to build an organization with them."[35] Lipowski is living proof that no matter its object, tenacity is contagious. If you can truly communicate your devotion to your particular artistic cause, others are sure to join you in supporting it.

★ ★ **KEYNOTES** ★ ★

Questions to Ask Yourself

- Am I succumbing to mission creep? Is the daily struggle for financial survival or the need to solve smaller problems as they arise, either for me or my organization, keeping me from seeing and working toward my long-term goals? Are there any risks I am not taking because I am afraid of losing what I have already achieved?

- Are there any performers or ensembles, in America or abroad, who are doing what I want to do or something similar? What can I learn from their success?

- Are gaps in my knowledge preventing me from working toward my goals? (In order to chart a course, you have to know not only the end point but also where on the map you are right now. For performers, that's a combination of artistic skills, financial health, management and leadership skills, the strength of your vision, and the quality and extent of your professional network. Some of these areas may be strong. Some of these areas may be underdeveloped. To make real progress, you have to get real about where you or your group measure up and where you don't. Be fearless in your self-assessment, and you'll be all the better equipped to meet future challenges.)

- Am I overworking myself? (Not putting in your time will destroy your chances of success in any field, but so too will putting in too much time. There is a point in all endeavors when effort becomes counterproductive. It is impossible to do good work if you don't give yourself some time to step back and renew your energy and interest.)

- How do I find my niche? Here are some helpful questions:
  - —How do others consistently describe me?
  - —What makes me odd or different from my peers?
  - —Is there a persistent, unsolved problem facing my peers in the performing arts community? (Solving it yourself, or collaborating with others to solve it, could uncover a niche that you could fill. By making a valuable contribution to your profession, you might also make a place for yourself in it.)

Tips

- Write down a succinct description of your vision in a place where you can regularly look at it, like a note on a digital device or a piece of paper you carry with you. If you are feeling discouraged or tired, take a quick break and reread your vision. Do the same thing on a day when you're feeling energized and effective, to connect your vision to a sense of momentum and well-being. As we've said elsewhere, in the arts it is not the promise of financial reward that keeps us moving but dedication to a higher vision.
- Many performing arts organizations in Europe are still generously state-funded. Consider spending some time abroad after graduation. It can provide you with a steady income as well as give your credentials some added pedigree.

Exercises

- **Vision and goals.** In a single phrase, write down the long-term vision you have for your career or your organization. For example: "An award-winning soprano who has performed leading roles in opera houses in Europe and the United States." Now, in the form of past-tense sentences, write down intermediate goals that will help you achieve your vision. For example: "I have taken a master class with Renée Fleming," "I have gone to 15 auditions this spring," or "I have sung a series of solo recitals, including works especially composed for me." Now, in between your intermediate goals, write down even smaller goals. For example: "I have asked friends and colleagues to recommend potential agents," or "I have emailed my composer friend to see if he is interested in collaborating on a recital series." Make the goals as small and achievable as you need to. The magic of this exercise is that it helps you directly connect the actions you are taking today with the larger, more distant vision you have for your career. All of us do better when we are motivated by a sense of purpose and when we feel that our daily actions are connected to that sense of purpose. And one of the easiest ways to get unstuck is to know exactly what small, achievable, but meaningful action is the right one to take next.

- **Distribution of responsibility.** (This is for small ensembles of performers who don't have full-time managers.) Try the exercise that Christopher Dylan Herbert used (as described earlier in this chapter). Take a sheet of paper and divide it up equally into sections, one for each member of your group. In each section, list the administrative duties of each member. Are the lists visually unbalanced? Are some a lot longer than others? If yes, discuss how to balance out the sections or to keep the current distribution with a clear understanding of why. Is there duplication of responsibilities among the lists? Are there essential tasks that aren't in anybody's column? Are there tasks that need to move regularly from one member to the next? If you're doing this exercise in a group, make a collective effort to keep the discussion positive. In listing everybody's responsibilities, don't focus the discussion on blaming some people for what they're not doing. Use this exercise to refine a balanced, positive vision that the whole group can work together toward achieving.

- **Book a performance today.** That's right, we want you to go out and book a performance today somewhere in your community! Juilliard

Professor Bärli Nugent has an exercise she springs on her students during her career development seminar. She asks them to leave campus for two hours and come back having booked a concert somewhere in New York City. The students start out shocked and convinced of their inevitable failure, but they always come back successful. They don't book concerts at Carnegie Hall or in big Broadway theaters, but instead in coffee shops, the back rooms of bars, community centers, stores, art galleries, or other crazy out-of-the-way places. In every place, they discover people who are excited about hosting a live performance. The point, says Nugent, is to get her students to realize that the opportunity to share their art and start building an audience is everywhere around them, if they're just willing to look for it. Don't hesitate to try out this exercise with a friend or colleague. You can bounce ideas off one another and help give each other the courage to go outside your comfort zone. If pianist Andrew Shapiro (see Chapter 10) can advance his career by performing in a McDonald's, it's worth it to search your community for overlooked opportunities.

FUNDRAISING

by William F. Baker

This subject, while it seems difficult and nuanced, is in many ways the easiest to master—to raise funds, you just have to ask! It may not be as simple as "ask and ye shall receive," but it's a sure thing that if you don't ask, you won't receive. It is amazing how many people stew about asking for financial assistance, don't do it, and then say they are having difficulty getting support. Why does this happen? The answer, of course, is that most of us find it hard to do. We feel like supplicants or think for some social reason that it's not right to ask directly for help.

In fact, though, most of our requests are not for ourselves but for a greater good in which we may be the creator or a principal participant. That's important to remember. The request is not for you! It's for something that will enrich the lives of others in society.

To succeed at something as complex as fundraising takes some understanding and discipline. But mostly, it requires your authenticity and passion for the subject, as well as some hard work. Many arts professionals I know spend the majority of their time in their early years raising money. It's a serious and time-consuming enterprise. Know that if you're going after a career in the not-for-profit performing arts world, fundraising is part of the bargain.

I spent many decades in the commercial television business and never thought about the subject of fundraising. I did spend a great deal of time doing business deals and promoting and selling our services to other broadcasters. But fundraising as practiced in the not-for-profit world was the furthest thing from my mind. In fact, when charities approached me for donations, I was sometimes bothered and didn't understand the need (maybe because it was never well explained).

When I changed careers and got into public TV, my world changed. Now the shoe was on the other foot and I had to get support for our operations. I was very frightened at first of the prospect of asking others for money and worried about my ability to make it happen. But I was under pressure to raise millions of dollars, so I had no choice but to get about it. The welfare of my staff and my whole organization depended on the gifts I had to solicit. Luckily for me, I was not starting a small, entrepreneurial charity, so I was blessed with considerable resources at the station and some great teachers. I also had the public television brand to precede me into every one of my fundraising interactions, which was a huge help.

My first break came when our major gift fundraiser set me up to meet with a wealthy, generous man who loved our work. He really wanted to join the board. I told him we'd be honored to have him on our board but needed some help. I asked, "Would you be willing to give us a $1 million gift?" (Of course, you shouldn't ask someone for $1 million if he doesn't have it. Prospect research is always one of the first steps in fundraising.) He said yes, and that gave me the confidence to go out and raise more large gifts. I have been credited with raising $1 billion for New York's PBS station during my 20 years there, but that happened only because we had a great product and a great support staff. Without that foundation, my efforts would have fallen far short of what they eventually achieved. I'll never forget that first big gift, though. It was a cause for celebration and a wonderful confidence builder, as you will see when you get whatever amount feels like your first big donation.

One of my very best fundraising teachers was Larry Lynn, who became my VP of development at New York PBS, having recently come from the senior fundraising position at American Ballet Theatre. (His essay on fundraising appears later in this chapter.) Larry was a great teacher about the art of fundraising. He made it clear that while he could provide the tools and understanding, in the end, major fundraising had to be done by the head of the organization—who is the one person who has the positional platform, the operating control, and the *vision* that major donors require. Top donors usually don't want to hear from fundraisers. They want to speak directly to principals in the organization, who can assure them of how their money will be spent and have the leadership abilities to make an organization thrive.

So be careful if a "professional fundraiser" comes to you and suggests that she can raise money for your organization if you hire her. First, you should know that, while not illegal, it's considered unethical for a fundraiser to operate on a commission basis (taking a percentage of the money raised). Second, in small organizations, it rarely pays to have a salaried fundraiser. The additional money raised is usually consumed by fundraising overhead and salaries, leaving little left over to benefit the mission.

In a small, nonprofit arts organization, the fundraising responsibility falls in the laps of the performers and the director. In many ways that's good, because you have a chance to develop and nurture the connections that may enable you to grow the donations, as you'll sense what givers are really interested in. And once you get over your fears of asking directly, you'll find that it's an adventure to win the gifts, make worthwhile things happen with the money, and share your successes with your donor! It pays as well to share your failures—you have to be honest with everyone who is willing to donate to your cause. If you are authentic and truthful about your work, you'll be amazed at how much tolerance donors have for failure. If your relationship with them is open and honest, they'll know from you how hard you are trying. Sharing failures with your funders can actually be a source of strength, because they are often eager to share their opinions about how your organization can make changes to be successful. Those with the resources to make major donations also tend to be people with incredible connections that they are often willing to make on behalf of your organization, which can be just as valuable as contributions of money.

THE BOARD OF DIRECTORS

Both for-profit and nonprofit organizations have boards of directors. For both types of organizations, this group of people is often the key to success or failure. Why? In for-profit organizations, board members supply strategic guidance, select the CEO, approve budgets, make connections with other businesses, and help the CEO keep the business focused. In nonprofit businesses, they do much the same, but with one key difference. They are usually the lead and major financial supporters. In nonprofits, the board's main role is to "give or get!" This means that they either have to give a certain amount of money, or go out and get it. This doesn't mean the board can ignore the general creative and business function of your company, but the money issue is paramount. As artistic or executive director of your own organization, you probably don't need creative or artistic help at this point (though a willingness to listen to others, especially those willing to support you, will never steer you wrong). What you really need is money! This is not all bad. Many founding board members are excited about seeing their money and their efforts help create something new.

To reiterate, *when you ask for money you are not begging for money for yourself. You're asking for the economic resources to make something wonderful happen for society.*

The ideal starting board size is around ten people, but any size will do. In the beginning, a small board (between five and ten) is easier to handle and manage. Large nonprofits often have huge boards, sometimes more than 50 people, because of the high demands of fundraising. Finding these board members is often a challenge. Some individuals who are willing to support you may not understand or want the responsibility of board membership. Be careful of "inbreeding"; that is, avoid having family members on your board. Don't get frustrated when you have trouble locating new board members. Find an excited, wealthy, and experienced leader to be your chair, and he will help recruit the others. You might worry that your board could become a purely social enterprise—an excuse to party and have fun. I wouldn't worry about that. There's nothing wrong with socializing as long as the mission is not compromised and the tail doesn't start wagging the dog.

All the issues I have outlined must be carefully thought through. Ask friends, family, and trusted professionals for advice.

The ideal board has a chair who is a powerful, wealthy, or highly connected and well-regarded person who brings in her friends and stays out of the director's creative hair. Such persons are out there and can be found. That's why developing a network of your own is so valuable. You'll likely be able to do this if you work hard and are patient.

An alternative to what I have suggested is a "pure board" of top professional people who have the expertise you need and care about the mission of your charity—big-name musicians or dancers or actors who are willing to lend their names and offer advice to your organization. Of course, this would be wonderful. Many times, however, such people are too busy to attend meetings. And despite their wealth, they are rarely eager to part with their own money. So in all likelihood, you will still need a wealthy chair who is prepared to donate or has friends who will. It can be easier to get such persons if your board is peppered with big, credible talents.

Items related to boards of directors include liability insurance, without which you will not attract senior people; suitable meeting locations and facilities, which often can be borrowed from corporations for free; and legal assistance. Lawyers can be very expensive. There are lawyers, though, who are willing to donate their services to cash-strapped worthy causes, and that's what you need. Incidentally, they also make good board members!

There are organizations in some communities and at some law schools that have not-for-profit help divisions to work with worthy start-up charities. All should be investigated when you are looking for the best people for your board.

FOUNDATIONS

Foundations are a traditional and trusted source of funds. We've all heard the names of the big ones: Gates, Ford, Carnegie, MacArthur, Mellon, and others. Don't pin all your hopes on support from major foundations at the outset, as there is a long line of more mature organizations in front of you. But it's never too early in your career to start trying. Remember the example of Claire Chase (see Chapter 7), recipient of the most prestigious and famous foundation grant of all, a MacArthur "genius" award? It took three years and a string of 44 rejected applications before she won her first grant! To get started, consult foundationcenter.org and guidestar.org. Both are good, free sources of information and important data about foundations and how they give.

Every foundation has its own giving criteria. You can't ask a foundation that gives money for medical causes to fund your dance company, for example. You have to do your homework and ask the right foundation for the proper gift. Each foundation usually has its particular manner of accepting requests for funds. Some do not accept requests at all. All this needs to be researched using the aforementioned websites and other sources. It's best if you have a chance to actually meet program officers in your field to get advice and insight. (These are people with expertise in a given field who advise the foundations they work for on where to direct grants.) But sometimes cold applications work fine, too.

Don't get discouraged if your early attempts don't bear fruit. I've found about a 10 to 1 ratio of rejects to acceptances for grant applications. Your chances greatly improve if you know an officer or board member at the foundation. There are big advantages to asking local foundations to support local causes, since they have a commitment to the local community and often realize the power and importance of the performing arts to their area.

With foundations there's always a lot of paperwork, so accept it and be prepared for it. After you consult their websites and look them up online at sites like guidestar.org, you need to jump through all the hoops the institutions require. This takes time and effort. Remember that you will have many rejections, so it's best to ask at a number of foundations. If you succeed, you will have to follow up with a report about how you spent their money.

Sometimes a foundation will give you a "restricted gift," which is a sum of money that can be spent only in a certain way or on a certain project. Be careful to spend this restricted money as specified (not for general operations), keeping good records about how the money was spent.

Working with foundations can require a large investment of time and energy. Many performing arts leaders spend more than 50 percent of their time working on fundraising! Again, don't expect fundraising to be anything but serious, time-consuming work. But it's *you*, the leader of the company, whom supporters want to deal with, and it's *you* who has the vision.

KICKSTARTER AND OTHER CROWDFUNDING SITES

Kickstarter is only the most famous of a growing number of crowd-sourcing, or crowdfunding, websites out there. While the process varies on each site, the basics are the same. You create a page for your project that has a pitch, usually a video and some images and text, telling people why they should donate. There might be various rewards associated with different levels of funding. Then people are invited to give over a specific period of time via the site. At the end of the period of time, you have either achieved full funding for your project or not.

Here are some key things to consider if you're thinking about building a Kickstarter page or something similar for your project:

1. **Don't expect the site to do the work of publicizing your project.** There are stories of some projects that have gone viral and achieved orders of magnitude more funding than they needed. These projects are the exception rather than the rule, so don't make having a viral hit your plan. Instead, do everything you can to promote your project in other ways: social media, word of mouth, fundraising events, celebrity endorsements, and institutional partnerships. These traditional ways of raising money are still powerful and can still get you where you need to be.

   It is best to think of your Kickstarter page not as the main engine of your fundraising campaign but instead as a kind of promotional tool that doubles as a donation service. Whenever you talk to potential donors about your project, show them your crowdfunding web page. It will give them something to remember, a concrete way to interact with your project, and also a convenient way to tell others about it.

2. **Give people a reason to look at your crowdfunding web page.** This doesn't have to be the same as the reason to give money to

your project. For example, your project might be a jazz concert series for young, undiscovered composers and players, but your video might be a personal appeal from Wynton Marsalis. People are going to watch your video to see Wynton Marsalis, not because they care right off the bat about your idea, and that's okay. Find a way to make your appeal interesting in its own right. Consider hiring a copywriter to spruce up the language of your appeal or some pro videographers or animators to make a high-quality video. If you can, get somebody famous to do the talking for you. Be creative in thinking of eye-catching ways to get your message across.

3. **Seek out partnerships with people and institutions who can help you get the word out.** Kickstarter and other similar sites are partnering with institutions to curate online lists of campaigns. For example, as of this writing, Public Radio Exchange has a page hosted on the Kickstarter site listing projects the group likes, including podcasts, radio shows, documentaries, and even a graphic novel. Potential donors who already know and trust Public Radio Exchange are likelier to give money to these projects. Other institutions with curated lists on Kickstarter as of this writing are the Sundance Institute, the Rhode Island School of Design, HotDocs, Yale University, and even the city of Chicago.

Find a community organization or institution that you think might want to help your project, contact the people there, and see if they might be interested in promoting your project. If they don't have a curated list on your crowdfunding website, suggest that they make one. And it goes without saying that if you can get celebrities to lend their name, image, or voice to your project, do it. Don't be afraid to ask anyone and everyone, no matter how famous, especially if what you're doing is not-for-profit.

4. **Before you start, have people ready to step in and fully fund you at the 11th hour.** Most crowdfunding sites don't allow partially funded projects. That means that if you don't reach 100 percent of your projected funding in the established time frame, you don't get any of the money you raised, even if you are just a little bit short. This can be demoralizing for you and your funders, as well as a waste of your considerable time and effort. The best solution is to have one or more donors waiting in the wings, willing to donate up to the full amount you need at the last minute. It makes everybody else who donated feel better, but more important, it ensures that you get to keep the rest of what you raised. This has become a standard best practice in online fundraising, but it's best not to advertise that you're doing it, or else people might not be motivated to give to your project in the first place.

5. **Consider the scope of your project before you decide if online crowdfunding is right for you.** As online crowdfunding matures as a way of raising capital or collecting donations, it is becoming clear that some projects are just too big to succeed in this format. If you're making a short film, a concert series, or some other small to midlevel project that requires anywhere from, say, $300 to $3,000, experience shows that online crowdfunding works. If you're trying to fund something that requires more money, chances are you're not going to be able to attract enough donors to make it work.

John Fox, an Emmy- and Peabody-winning TV producer friend of mine, did succeed in raising $141,000 on Kickstarter for Onstage America, a project that would film outstanding local theater across the country for broadcast on PBS. Fox had the backing of eight A-list celebrities, including Meryl Streep and John Lithgow. The pitch video showed some hilarious banter between superstars David Hyde Pierce and Lewis Black. The project received numerous social media plugs (including one from the theater critic of the *Wall Street Journal*) and was officially backed by PBS, which is America's most trusted and widely known media brand. And yet, Fox and his colleagues were only able to raise just over their minimum of $125,000 by the skin of their teeth and at the last minute. Fox says it took a frantic marshaling of every resource he and his colleagues could think of to fund the project. The Kickstarter page was a great thing to show people, he says, but it didn't do any of the work of promoting the project. That was entirely left to Fox and his colleagues, and they ended up achieving it through good old-fashioned personal networking.

When Fox told a professional fundraiser about his 30-day scrambling together of media coverage, and donations from friends, friends of friends, and celebrities, the fundraiser said, "Oh, that's a capital campaign, just like one I'd create for a huge institution, just compressed into one month!"

The takeaway for online crowdfunding is this: Think of it as a new, accessible, and potentially useful tool. But be sure your project is the right size, and have support and a backup plan in place before you begin. And, if you can, try to have fun with it and learn as much as you can!

FRIENDRAISING

In the end, finding money for your work is basically dependent upon having a network of friends who can give or get. Cultivating such friends is a process that professionals call *friendraising*. Here are some examples of how it's done.

Never stage a performance without getting to know the folks who came to see you at the after-event. This is fundamental! Also, solicit email addresses from those who attend your performances. In the process of friendraising, be yourself, be real, and be authentic. You'd be amazed at how many people want to meet you. Even the richest, most powerful folks are always amazed and impressed with people like you who exhibit great talent and discipline. They wish they could do what you do!

It takes time and great creativity to find places where you can meet people who can help you. The good news is that they are out there, and not just in the big cities. Every community has people of means who might be willing to lend their support. Often, attending the fundraising events of larger, mature performing arts institutions is a good place to start building your network. It might seem hard to just walk up to strangers and introduce yourself, but don't worry: You don't have to ask them for money right then and there. On a first meeting, you are just trying to connect. You can talk about the event, and the guests are likely to ask you about what you are doing—a great chance to get them interested in your project. And don't forget to listen. Performing arts events attract an interesting crowd. Make an effort to learn what people's interests and abilities are. You might meet a potential donor who isn't interested in what you do but could support the work of one of your friends or colleagues. The more people you know, the more you are in a position to make good things happen for everybody, not just yourself, and that is the true secret to long-term success and a greater level of happiness and fulfillment in your career. When you build your own network of friends and supporters, you are also supporting a larger, interconnected network that is bigger than just you and your projects. When you have a chance to help others, listen to that voice inside you that says it's worth the time and effort to do so.

Above all, don't get discouraged. In your search for water, you will end up digging dry holes. Again, have fun and learn a lot. There are many nice, interesting, and generous folks out there. You will connect with the right ones, given time.

EVENTS AND GALAS

Inevitably, someone will say you should have a fundraising event or party. But it's not always the way to go. In fact, even the most sophisticated charities sometimes do events that end up losing money. You must be careful of the big costs of gala events: drinks, food, invitations, and facilities. Conversely, events can be a terrific way to network. So this area is quite nuanced. Sometimes throwing your own event is the right move, and sometimes it isn't. It all depends on your goals and where you are in developing your organization. And not every fundraising event has to be too lavish. In fact, if you're a new organization specializing in experimental performing art, for example, a lavish or traditional event might not be what people expect. So, when deciding whether to throw your own event, you have to factor in costs versus your fundraising goals, potential side benefits like networking or press coverage, and the public image of your organization that you want to put out there.

Sometimes collaborating with another organization or a venue can give you many of the benefits of throwing an event without having to shoulder all the hassle and costs of doing it on your own. For example, a restaurant might be having an opening or an event and you can trade a small performance for visibility and a chance to circulate. The same goes for galleries, retail establishments, or other charitable institutions that are outside the arts, like hospitals and medical groups.

An important thing to think about is some basic accounting—the difference between gross and net. This is critical. *Gross* means the entire revenue for the event—all the money received at the fundraiser. *Net* means the money left over after you pay all your expenses. Of course, you can never be certain in advance of any net income! A mistake even big charities sometimes make is to think only about gross. You hear people working at a big symphony say they had a gala and made "a million dollars," when that is the gross and not the net. Often, fundraisers publicize gross income without accounting for how much it cost to generate that income. Typically, the amount left over is about 50 percent of the gross. So watch event costs carefully! Don't make commitments with event fundraisers unless you have an escape route to cancel the event without penalty if things start looking too expensive. Don't make nonrefundable advance payments for the rental of facilities unless you are absolutely sure you'll have enough people coming to your event.

Homes of board members are possible sites to consider. Often, wealthy board members are eager to have parties in their own homes and to highlight their charitable interests. The board members pay for the event, so any donations are almost pure profit.

Keep your antennae up for unforeseen costs and difficulties associated with fundraising events and galas. Many times, it's hard to get people to an event when there are so many worthy causes and events competing for the time and attention of wealthy individuals. That's why it's best to have the correct folks on your board so they can use their powerful networks and relationships to get your work in front of the best people.

So that's my take on fundraising. I've been credited with raising a great deal of money, but like all team efforts, I've stood on the shoulders of giants. For example, Paula Kerger, now president and CEO of PBS in Washington, D.C., was my VP of development at WNET, New York City's PBS member station. She was brilliant and very strategic and had been head of major gifts for the Metropolitan Opera.

The person who got me going in fundraising and gave me my best training was Larry Lynn, a sophisticated fundraiser who worked for American Ballet Theatre, NYU Medical Center, and other charities. He's the very best in my opinion. Larry, who is now a top consultant, shares his thoughts with you in the rest of this chapter.

TIPS FROM LARRY LYNN,
A PROFESSIONAL FUNDRAISER

If you've turned to this chapter, I congratulate you on your fortitude, courage, and determination. Over the last 44 years, I've raised money for a broad spectrum of organizations including ballets, hospitals, medical research organizations, higher education, public broadcasting, museums, social services, groups supporting the disabled, and many more. Without qualification, raising funds for the performing arts was by far the hardest.

Before we go further, let me tell you a little bit about myself. I started my fundraising career in the early 1970s at a service organization that was home to innovative dance, theater, and music groups, including some of great fame like Alwin Nikolais, Murray Louis, the Open Theater, the Living Theatre, the Manhattan Project, the Gene Frankel Theatre Workshop, and Multigravitational Aerodance Group. I served on the board of directors of the last one for many years, and it gave me great perspective on what the other side of the table in fundraising was like. I ran fundraising at American Ballet Theatre (ABT) during most of the years when Mikhail Baryshnikov was artistic director, from 1979 to 1987. I have also been an unpaid adviser or compensated consultant to several small dance companies. In this section I discuss two of the three kinds of performing arts organizations. The first are *presenting organizations* like the Kennedy Center, the Adrienne Arsht Center, and the Roundabout Theatre. You can call these presenting/producing organizations because most of them do both, but here I call them presenting organizations. The second type are *content organizations*, like ABT (my home for eight years), the New York Philharmonic, the Chicago Symphony, the Lyric Opera of Chicago, the Paul Taylor Dance Company, American Conservatory Theater, and so many more (thank God). The third type are *service organizations* like Theatre Development Fund, Alliance for the Arts, and Business Council for the Arts. Here, I deal with the first two. Service organizations are the hardest to raise money for, for reasons that will become obvious.

Sometimes these distinctions become blurred. The Metropolitan Opera is both a presenting organization and America's greatest opera company. When the opera is not performing, the Met goes into its presenting mode, its venue offering the works of American Ballet Theatre and many content providers. ABT has performed as a Met Opera presentation for 40-plus years every spring. So you can look at the Met two ways: It is an opera company that has its own house, and it is a presenting house that has its own opera company. Lincoln Center, where the Metropolitan Opera House is located, is rife with blurred distinctions. It is a presenter of certain programs, like the Mostly Mozart Festival, but it is principally a landlord that leaves the producing/presenting/performing to its tenants, referred to as "constituents," like the Metropolitan Opera, New York City Ballet, New York Philharmonic, Film Society, and Lincoln Center Theater.

Each of the three different types of performing arts organizations described above has its own strategic advantages and disadvantages, and understanding what they are—and capitalizing on that understanding—is the essence of what we are about to discuss. Before we go into it, though, it's important to understand the principal sources of contributed funds.

FUNDING SOURCES

The superficial distinction most people make about funding sources includes individuals, foundations, corporations, and government. To simplify, there are two categories of individuals: those who make major gifts, and those whom we call "members," who make modest, renewable gifts. I am not treating foundations as distinct from individuals. In a discussion of performing arts funding, foundations behave like major gift individuals, except for their penchant for paperwork. The giving of a foundation to the arts reflects either the interests of the founder or the enthusiasms of the current trustees and/or senior staff. I am not going to spend much time on corporate giving since so much has already been said on this topic; a quick history lesson suffices.

I began my career in the early 1970s. Back then, corporations routinely made gifts of a purely altruistic nature. That changed in the 1980s for two reasons. First, the pool of money available for donations was drained away by the higher salaries of executives and by the debt resulting from mergers and acquisitions activities. Second, there was a growing obsession with what American Express coined "cause-related marketing." Corporations increasingly saw funds given to charities as an extension of their marketing budgets. This was not a brand-new idea. Texaco had sponsored the Met Opera radio broadcasts for years, and PBS had enlisted ExxonMobil and others as "underwriters." Transactional funding (i.e., the expectation that companies would receive a marketing boost or other favors in return for donations) had always been there, but it exploded in the 1980s.

This gave performing arts organizations an advantage over many other types of charities. We all began to "sell" whatever we could, e.g., open rehearsals, galas, national tours, city engagements, and direct marketing programs. The sports world provided a template that many of us followed for corporate naming opportunities. Of the two types of performing arts organizations described above, the content organizations had glamour and star power on their side. The presenting organizations had glamour as well, and the added benefit of a fixed venue. ABT had two big successes in the 1980s with corporate sponsorship. For three years, we had Moët Hennessy sponsoring our galas across the country to promote its Dom Pérignon brand. We also enlisted Movado in our city-by-city marketing efforts. The chair and founder of Movado joined the board of trustees, and this relationship continued for many years.

INDIVIDUAL GIVING

The heart of performing arts fundraising is individual giving. Let's begin with what I call the "first premise": They don't support you if they don't consume you. This is not true of all charities. For example, people support health charities, veterans' organizations, social services, and others without consuming their services. When was the last time you directly benefited from the American Red Cross or the Salvation Army? When it comes to higher education or religion, we tend to support those we have a stake in. With the performing arts, you are highly unlikely to get a gift from someone who hasn't attended at least several performances. The more frequently they attend, the more likely they are to support you at some level.

When I first arrived at ABT, I came with a strong background in direct mail fundraising. The list brokers (businesses that trade in lists of addresses tailored to meet marketing needs) had snowed the ABT staff into renting the lists of *Town & Country* or *Forbes* magazine subscribers or purchasers of expensive cars. The theory was that rich people were more cultivated and more likely to support the ballet. This is not incorrect, but simplistic and costly. These lists consistently returned very little; the poor results were disguised by much better results from lists of ticket buyers that we traded for. At the time, ABT visited nine cities each year, presented by local performing arts venues like the Kennedy Center, the San Francisco Opera, and the Met Opera. We wrote it into all contracts with presenters that we were entitled to an electronic file of all single ticket and subscription buyers for our engagement, and we rented lists from them of attendees at other dance presentations. Our results soared.

Finding modest gift donors is easy if you are a good steward of your own attendance lists. Engaging and keeping them is the real challenge. At ABT, we offered two perquisites that were the bedrock of engagement and retention, and neither cost us significant dollars. First, we conducted one or more open rehearsals in each tour city. Donors of $40 and more could reserve two seats. We used dress rehearsals for this member benefit. These rehearsals would go on for hours, and donors felt they had gotten two free tickets in the orchestra to a performance for the cost of their membership. The second bedrock benefit of membership was advanced mailings of single seat and subscription tickets. Donors had a two-week window of opportunity to buy their tickets for our upcoming season before we opened up reservations to the general public. If you check the ABT website today, you still find these two bedrock benefits; the minimum price has changed to $90, but it's been 30 years since we bumped it from $35 to $40.

MAJOR DONORS

The first premise applies emphatically with major donors: If they're not already sitting in a seat, you are unlikely to convert them. Yes, there are rare exceptions, but this is a 99 percent valid premise, so please don't contact me about the exceptions. I've seen them close up. Most of the exceptions were once removed from an ardent fan, like a sibling, parent, or romantic companion. Let's deal not with the one-percenters but focus on the 99 percent.

The best place to find them is among current donors and ticket buyers. Today, at least a dozen vendors offer wealth screening services that allow you to run your lists of donors and ticket buyers against their database of wealth. The result is a list of your consumers with lots of financial data appended, like large stock holdings, real estate values, the size of their 401(k) plans, yacht ownership, and plane ownership. I've used these services with lists of anywhere from 5,000 to 400,000 names. They definitely work, but they are not perfect. Somehow, certain very rich people find ways to stay off these lists.

There are simple ways to develop major gift prospect lists on your own. Back in the 1980s, ABT was an early and aggressive adopter of computerization. We would take the Met Opera's ABT season ticket list and transpose it into a spreadsheet program. We would then sort by zip code and isolate some of the region's best, starting with the Upper East Side, the lower half of the Upper West Side, and New York suburbs like Scarsdale, Bedford, Great Neck, and Lawrence. We would get granular with street addresses, isolating, say, Central Park South. We extracted the lower numbers on Central Park West and the lowest numbers on the Upper East Side's numerical cross streets. If you don't know Manhattan, this means we isolated those who lived between Central Park and Lexington Avenue—the heart of the famed Upper East Side. We would even isolate specific buildings, usually famous New York co-ops like the San Remo or 850 Park Avenue.

Once we had the list of suspected wealthy ticket buyers, we would share the list with our board's development committee and the board as a whole. We gave each board member who lived in an apartment building the names of other tenants who turned up on our list. Through this primitive database marketing strategy, we were able to expand our major donor base quickly and substantially. It also helped us identify potential new board members.

The best way to engage a major donor is a two-part strategy. First, whenever possible, use a peer connection to begin the process. Wealthy individuals are more likely to give when asked by another wealthy person. Part of it is a reciprocity thing; they will turn around and solicit your board member for their favorite charity. Another part of it is social connectedness. If you have a board leader other wealthy people want to connect to, one easy way to do so is to become involved in his favorite charity. At ABT, we had the chair and CEO of PepsiCo as our board chair and Jacqueline Kennedy Onassis as our honorary gala chair. Every advertising agency, investment bank, and law firm in America wanted a piece of PepsiCo's business; I don't think I need to elaborate on the star power of Mrs. Onassis. You may be reading this in some small city in the middle of America and feeling helpless about your own circumstances. Don't! Every city, town, and village has its own version of Mr. PepsiCo and Mrs. Onassis. It's your job to identify and engage them. Sometimes you get to create your community's version of Mrs. Onassis. (That's the beautiful thing about New Money.)

The second part of engaging a major donor is deploying your artistic leadership. If you are unwilling to play a major role in fundraising, my advice to you is polish up your résumé. Some artistic directors are natural fundraisers. But others—especially those who are actively engaged as a dancer, musician, choreographer, etc.—feel they have done their part already, and fundraising is beneath their dignity. But you are kidding yourself if you think the rich people will overlook the eccentricities of an unsociable artistic director and will remain engaged purely because of their love for the art form. At some point, the artistic director needs to embrace potential major donors, or else they will find someone of similar stature who is more welcoming.

During my ABT years, we were not the only major dance company in New York City. I'll tell you a story about another one without identifying it by name. The company's artistic director, a formidable choreographer, would tell ABT's artistic director that he was so important he shouldn't have to play the fundraising game. He insisted he would never let himself be so engaged. How did the company get around this? The artistic director's partner in their company was a great man, and he (as I came to understand) had persuaded the artistic director that the people who made major gifts to their company were the artistic director's personal friends, not mere philanthropists. The artistic director had lunch and dinner regularly with the major donors. Often, they would bring friends along who also happened to be major gift prospects; however, in the artistic director's mind, these were his friends, and these social occasions were not about the money. But they were, of course.

Presuming you have a willing artistic director, it's your job to coach and direct her. You need to make sure she's gotten a short biography of the prospect. Since you presumably know what performances the prospect has attended, it's your job to make sure the artistic director knows that as well. Once the major donor is engaged, it's your job to make sure the artistic director sends a personal thank-you note for every gift, and a birthday card wouldn't hurt either. Of course, they are not really "friends," but it's your job to create a "virtual friendship."

Here are some of the engagement strategies that worked for us at ABT. We knew what performances major gift donors (and prospects) were attending, and we knew exactly where they would be sitting. We would call them in advance and ask if they'd like to go backstage during one of the intermissions. I always had a development staff person in the house, and one of us would fetch the major donors at the beginning of an intermission and escort them backstage. We had explained the reasons for all of this to the dancers and tech staff, and they were most accommodating. We would always alert the artistic director as well. Sometimes, we'd invite major donors to stay backstage for an act, having cleared this ahead of time. (It's one thing to have extra people backstage during a pas de deux, and another thing entirely during all of Act II of *Swan Lake*.) Dance lends itself to this more than theater. With theater, donors want to see the play from the audience. Dance lovers, however, often see the same production more than once, so the rare backstage observance of an act is appreciated. In addition, with theater, I've found that actors are especially chatty after the final curtain and that donors enjoy a leisurely backstage tour at the end of the performance of a play.

Another effective strategy played out during our galas in each tour city. Wealthy people buy whole tables, but filling them is often a chore. We asked donors if they'd be willing to set aside two seats for members of the company. We had a 90 percent success rate placing dancers at tables. We chose carefully; the biggest donors and prospects got the principal dancers. We learned, though, that the donors found even the least experienced corps de ballet dancers completely charming. Dancers, actors, and musicians are all great with donors, and I found they appreciated being included at these events, even after a long day of rehearsals and performances. We even had success seating some of our senior tech people with donors.

One last thought about using performances for fundraising: If you have decent free tickets, be generous with foundation staffers and corporate giving people. It's always better if you offer before they have to ask. In a similar vein, if you have to paper the house, drop a stack of tickets at the local business, medical, and law schools. Your successors will thank you someday.

PLANNED GIVING AND ENDOWMENTS

Planned gifts are a way for your members and modest donors to make substantial lifetime gifts through a variety of trusts and annuities, as well as wills and bequests. Presenting institutions are more likely to succeed at planned giving because of the appearance of permanence. One of the coauthors of this book, Dr. Baker, and I once called on an investment banker and proposed he give a gift of $5 million to WNET. He told us he'd have to think about it because when he thought of gifts of that magnitude, he envisioned hospitals, universities, and libraries. What they all have in common is real estate. In the mid-1980s, ABT almost went under during a prolonged labor dispute. While it was playing out, we in the administration thought about what ABT really was and how fragile it could be. We rented a warehouse for sets and costumes, rented a rehearsal space, and owned the rights to a few dozen ballets. That was it. It's much harder to raise endowment funds or solicit planned gifts when your existence, no matter how august, is so insubstantial.

If you are a content organization, it is still worth trying to get things endowed. Use the higher education model of named professorships for positions like your artistic director, principal dancers, resident choreographer, first violin, conductor, principal pianist, and so on. Create named funds for ongoing functions, e.g., the New Choreography Fund, or the New Composers Fund. Look at what you already spend money on year in and year out. Repackage these into named funds, multiply the annual cost by 20, and you have an endowment proposal.

If you have a permanent venue, any wall, door, or space that doesn't have a plaque on it represents a fundraising failure. Every seat in the main theater should be named for someone. Somewhere prominent there should be a board or plaque for people to honor deceased loved ones. No grand piano is complete without a little brass plaque. It is the fashion accessory that says you, the fundraiser, are doing your job.

Consider everything nameable. When I ran development at NYU Medical Center, a donor asked if he could have his name on the hospital elevator. One day, I was crammed in it with a dozen other people, and I looked up at the polished brass plaque and smiled. It was probably the most frequently read plaque in the entire hospital. I went back to the same donor and got him to take a second elevator.

A WORD OR TWO ABOUT BOARDS

Boards are the best thing that happens to the arts fundraiser. Here's the catch: You have to manage them, not the other way around. When I first arrived at ABT, I asked the chair of the nominating committee how the process worked. He told me there wasn't one and asked if I had any suggestions. I offered to staff the committee, promising to provide them with a steady supply of prospects. At the time, we had great leadership, including Mr. PepsiCo, Mrs. Onassis, and some soon-to-be legendary Wall Street people; however, we also had a lot of legacy deadwood.

My staff began trolling the subscriber and gala attendee lists from all over the country. We had a number of objectives. First, we wanted one "anchor" trustee in each of the annual tour cities, places like Chicago, Los Angeles, Washington, D.C., and Miami. Second, we wanted New Yorkers capable of making really large gifts. Since our studios were in Manhattan and we performed at the Met Opera, donor cultivation could be year-round and efficient. We not only fed the nominating committee a list of targets of opportunity but also developed a comprehensive scorecard for current board members.

Based on this scorecard, the board leadership, with our gentle direction, developed a set of criteria for board membership, including a minimum annual gift, the purchase of a gala table in at least one city, and the understanding that there would soon be a capital campaign, and at that time each board member would be expected to make a one-time special gift. Over the next three years, we weeded about a third of the board, but we replaced them with people who could give and get effectively. We also established strong gala committees in each of the target tour cities. When I left ABT after more than eight years to go to WNET, board development was my proudest achievement.

A UNIQUE BUT WORTHY CHALLENGE

It's really hard raising money for the performing arts. It is easier to raise funds in other areas. For example, it was easy when I was raising funds at NYU Medical Center for wheelchair-bound children and disabled vets. In public television (a challenge in itself), we owned our own television station, the glamour and visibility of which is a gift to fundraising at every level. At NYU Medical Center, we had rich old men with prostate and heart disease, as well as a steady stream of grateful patients of every stripe. When I consulted in higher education, we had alumni who had enjoyed probably the best years of their lives during college, and they had a vested interest in keeping the college brand strong. At ABT, we had that narrow sliver of people who loved the art of ballet, and only a sliver of that sliver had lots of money. When

I was interviewed by the board chair for my job at NYU Medical Center, I had already met with the staff. He asked me how NYU's development office differed from ABT's. I told him that at ABT, the CFO would periodically come bursting into my office and inform me that if I didn't come up with another $100,000 before week's end, we couldn't make the dancers' payroll. He laughed and offered me the job. Performing arts fundraising is about high stress and very long hours. I would leave the Met Opera after a performance and catch a train that would get me home before midnight, then return to my desk by 9 the next morning because that's when the board members would call. But when that curtain went up for the first act of *Swan Lake* and I felt I was truly a part of that moment, it was all worth it. It still moves me to think about those days.

★ ★ KEYNOTES ★ ★

Questions to Ask Yourself

- Do I know anybody who might be willing to be on my board of directors? Is there anybody in my network with skills, connections, or means who might be willing to help, or help me find others who are?
- Is online fundraising right for my organization? Are there certain projects that might be the right fit for an online campaign, while others might be too big? Is there a person with experience in online fundraising whom I can consult?
- Do I keep an email list of people who attend my performances? Could I be putting this to use for fundraising purposes?
- Are there any naming opportunities in my organization? (Regular activities, like annually scheduled performances, newly commissioned works, or educational activities, can all be named after individuals who or organizations that agree to fund them.)

Tips

- When asking for money, be assertive but don't be aggressive. Being assertive means that you are open and unambiguous about your intention to seek support. Everybody appreciates having a clear sense of the intentions of the people they're working with. Being aggressive means being overly confrontational and pushing your needs and desires at every possible moment. While an aggressive approach may win you a gift or two, it is unlikely to create positive, long-term relationships with donors.

- Never forget that when you're asking for money, even for an organization you may have founded and currently head up, you are not really asking for yourself. You are asking on behalf of the art you make and the audiences and larger community who are enriched by it.

- When looking for help for potential board members or those with legal and accounting skills (or those who might fulfill both roles), be sure to check out the professional schools and associations in your area. Law schools and business schools have clinics that are designed to give professional students real-world experience. Some, like the law clinic at Fordham University, even have specific programs devoted to helping people in the arts. Professional associations can also help get the word out that your organization needs assistance.

- Curious to know where to start looking for funding? Attend the performance of an established local theater, dance troupe, or musical ensemble and check the program to see who supports them.

- If you are looking for suggestions for making up your start-up board of directors, in this chapter, we've talked a lot about the ideal board members to supercharge your organization. But nobody is going to have that right out of the gate. Whom should you start with? Consider asking:

    —Somebody who cares deeply about what you do

—Somebody who has a lot of ties to the community

—Somebody with means (a polite way of saying "somebody who's rich")

—Somebody with skills you need, like public relations, law, or accountancy

- Never go to a fundraising meeting empty-handed. Always have a brochure, a business plan, a stack of glossy postcards, or even a link to a Kickstarter page or your home page (bring a computer or tablet with you so you can show off the page in the meeting) to show that your idea is for real and is already unfolding in the real world. People are much more willing to support work already under way than an idea.

Exercises

- Practice making "the ask." Asking for money can be an uncomfortable thing to do. You have to have a sense of when the moment is right, and you have to be able to gauge the temperament and interests of the potential donors you are working with. Depending on your level of access to potential donors, you may have only a few or even just one chance to ask for contributions. You want to be prepared enough so that you can be relaxed, authentic, and in-the-moment during your meeting, not worrying about what to say or how you or they are going to respond. So take a friend or another person from your organization and rehearse making the ask. It might seem a little silly, but have fun with this exercise. Put in some time to try out different approaches, and listen to what sounds good and what sounds bad when you say it.

- Pick a foundation and take a look at its online resources, as well as at information about the group offered on sites like GuideStar. Most major foundations have multiple areas of grant-making activity that are presided over by officers with expertise in that area. Take a look at past grants the foundation has given. Read the director's bio to learn what her interests are. Foundation directors have a major say in where the resources of their organizations are directed. Take a look at any resources the foundation offers for free to potential grantees or to nonprofits that work in its grant areas. Foundations often have excellent pages full of useful Web links for potential grantees or that are just offered for the benefit of the public. And if, in the course of this exercise, you have questions that the Web cannot answer, don't be afraid to email a program officer or somebody else at a foundation with questions. It could be the start of something big!

AUDITIONS, AGENTS, AND ANGELA'S STORY

Here we tackle two subjects that all serious performers will want to know more about. Auditions can be painful, but they don't have to be. And it is impossible to have a career without auditioning. It is worth it to learn how best to approach the process.

Agents can be invaluable, but before you rush out to get one, it helps to know when it is best to get one, how to find a good one, and what to expect when you have one.

The information in this chapter, as well as the story of Angela (the daughter of one of the authors) and her journey to Broadway and beyond, will be of particular value to actors. But as with all parts of this book, the insights here can be adapted to the needs of any performer.

AUDITIONS AND HOW TO HANDLE THEM

Auditions are an essential part of every performer's work. The key word in that sentence is *work*. Auditions need not be approached as stressful, unusual experiences or life-or-death trials. They can be seen merely as necessary tasks to be completed in the course of your career as a performing artist. In fact, if approached with the right attitude, auditioning can be an enjoyable and rewarding activity its own right. For actors especially, auditioning has to become part of your routine.

But having a good attitude about one of the most notorious parts of the performer's life is easier said than done. Here are a few tips to help you cultivate the right attitude and avoid some common mistakes.

We owe most of these insights to Dustin Flores and Paula Poeta, agents at the New York–based boutique talent agency The Mine, as well as Diane Wittry, who has heard countless auditions as the conductor of the Allentown Symphony Orchestra.

DON'T TAKE AUDITIONS PERSONALLY

An audition is not a judgment of your total worth as a person or even as an artist. An audition is a job interview. It is a professional meeting where those in charge of a project or performing arts organization determine if you can meet their needs at a particular moment in time. It is possible to be talented and disciplined and give a near-perfect audition and still not be the right fit for a particular job.

In the case of an acting audition, the director, the producers, and the casting director have a huge job on their hands each time they try to put together a cast. It is like fitting together a jigsaw puzzle composed of the budget, the parts already cast, the production deadline, and the particular vision of the director and his creative team. As an auditioner, you probably won't see the whole puzzle and where you might fit in. All you can do is show up and do your best. Take this as a comfort rather than a source of anxiety! Just keep the focus on doing your own work and you've got nothing else to worry about.

TAKE AUDITIONS SERIOUSLY,
BUT DON'T FREAK OUT ABOUT THEM, EITHER

Sure, that person on the other side of the table might be a huge Hollywood or Broadway producer, movie star, or virtuoso, but as far as the audition is concerned, she is just a businessperson looking to solve a problem. Movie stars and moguls are not gods but people with jobs to do, just like you. Help them do their job by showing up and giving them the best, most authentic audition you can give them.

By an authentic audition, we mean one in which you are totally focused on the work but also relaxed enough to let who you really are as a performer shine through. An audition usually consists of about two to three minutes of work, reading lines or playing notes in front of the people evaluating you. (Dance auditions can be longer and are partly undertaken in groups.) Don't give in to the temptation to dismiss the audition because it is only a few minutes of your life or, alternately, to imbue that short period of time with so much significance that you buckle under self-imposed pressure.

Don't be an over-rehearsed presentational robot, but don't let yourself get distracted or uninvested, either. Do everything you can to prepare for the audition, but once you are in it, relax and trust yourself. As Daniel Talbott discovered (see Chapter 7), a good actor always has a light touch. If you've done the work of preparation, you have nothing to worry about. In fact, in the moments of your audition, worry itself is your biggest enemy. Whatever the source of your worry, those who might hire you are likely to interpret worry or anxiety as signs of desperation or lack of experience. As with any job, people want to hire somebody who is dependable and unhindered by anxiety.

Focus on auditions as opportunities, not judgments. See them as sources of possibilities, not unpleasant trials. Confidence in your own preparation and a genuinely positive attitude toward the experience

188 THE WORLD'S YOUR STAGE

puts everybody in the room more at ease, starting with yourself. The better your performance, the more likely you are to stick in the mind of the casting director, even if you don't land the particular role in question.

BE ON TIME

This might seem obvious, but being late for auditions is a mistake that many aspiring performers actually make. Being on time is a huge part of the work of an audition. If you're late or cutting it close, you'll arrive flustered and not at your best. Worse, lateness is a signal to the people sitting on the other side of the table that you don't respect them or the work you're doing together. Remember, an audition is a job interview. In the corporate world, lateness would automatically remove you from the pool of candidates. Why should the performing arts world be any different?

So take some simple precautions and eliminate unnecessary worry from your experience. First, give yourself plenty of time to get from where you are to where the audition is taking place. Look up the directions the night before. And tack some extra time onto however much time you think you might need (or that an app says you might need) to get there.

Giving yourself plenty of time allows you to center yourself or calm down before it's your turn. You might even get a chance to do some chatting or networking beforehand with the other auditioners or members of the production or organization. Or you might need that extra time to make sure your instrument is in tune, find the right part of the building, or solve those other annoying problems that sometimes crop up.

Lay your clothes out the night before. For actors especially, showing up in clothes appropriate to the role can be a huge help. Don't wait until the morning of the audition to ask your agent or your coach about what outfit might enhance your chances of landing the part. This applies to dancers and instrumentalists as well. Choose clothes that let you be comfortable but also appropriately dressed. All of this preparation frees up your mind to focus on the important work at hand.

FOCUS ON AND ENJOY THE WORK—
DON'T JUST TRY TO LAND THE JOB

Just because you've chosen to respect an audition as work doesn't mean you can't also find fun and enjoyment in it. This is the performing arts, after all! Take pleasure in your two to three minutes of embodying the character, hitting the notes, or moving your body. Enjoying the actual work of performance rather than worrying about landing the job relieves some of the pressure and probably helps you perform better.

It also removes a potential block that many performers have toward auditioning in the first place. Statistically, any successful career is going to include a lot of auditioning, not all of it successful. It's best if you find a way to enjoy doing it, or better yet, even love doing it. It might not seem as enticing as performing before an audience, but auditioning is still a way for you to be of service to your chosen art form. Every audition, no matter the outcome, is valuable. It adds a little to the reservoir of your total personal experience. The more you love it, the more you'll do it. And the more you audition, the better your chances of getting work.

By enjoying the work, you're more likely to make a better impression on casting directors, who by their nature have long memories. It is their job to keep a mental catalog of all the performers who might someday be the right fit for a role in question. The first time you encounter a casting director, it's vital to make a good impression. Plus, the notes he is jotting down on the back of your head shot might be filed away and read weeks, months, or even years after the date of the audition. You want those notes to be positive.

As talent agent Paula Poeta says, "Book the room, don't book the job. The people on the other side of the table want you to do well. They are there as potential friends and fans, even if it turns out that you're not right for the job of the moment."[1]

DON'T TRY OUT NEW MATERIAL

An audition is not the place to workshop new material just because of the opportunity to get professional feedback. Use trusted friends, peers, a coach or agent, or your teachers for the job of evaluating your mastery of new material. An audition is always the place for your best work, period.

TREAT YOUR FELLOW AUDITIONERS AS COLLEAGUES, NOT ENEMIES

There is nothing wrong with using competition as motivation to do your best, but seeing your fellow performers as enemies rather than colleagues is a rookie mistake and likely to put you in a negative mindset. Any subset of the performing arts is a small community, and respecting all the people in it—whom you are likely to run into many, many times during your career—is always the best policy.

All of the talent agents, producers, directors, managers, and performing artists we spoke to in the course of writing this book articulated their own version of a "no jerks" policy. All things being equal, the performer who is going to make it out of the talent pool and into a job is going to be somebody who either has a reputation for being easy to work with or who radiates that mindset during her audition. There are enough competent and even exceptionally talented performers out there to make showing kindness and respect a serious edge. Plus, making friends with your fellow auditioners can sometimes pay off. During the final round of auditions for the TV show *The X-Files*, eventual costars David Duchovny and Gillian Anderson had an edge because they had struck up an acquaintance before the audition and offered to run lines with each other while waiting. The extra amount of ease and chemistry they established before the audition helped them land the roles that launched both their careers.[2]

SEE EVERY AUDITION AS A FRESH START

As a performer, there are no professional certifications or degrees that you can rely on to ensure your next job offer. Even that plum role in a movie or on a TV show, that seat in an orchestra or ensemble, or that time in a first-rate company is bound to end, and you will find yourself back in the audition pool. This is the nature of the performing artist's life, and it's best to find a way to embrace it rather than resent it.

To get that next job, you're going to have to prove yourself again! Try to see it as a fresh start rather than just having to start over. It can be scary to start over, but one of the joys of being a performer is that you get to start on one adventure after another. You're not chained to a desk and you don't have to show up at the same place, year in and year out. A life of frequent auditioning is a small price to pay for that freedom.

AGENTS: WHAT THEY DO AND HOW TO GET ONE

Agents are professionals whose job is to find you new work opportunities as a performer. They can also help you develop your talent and learn how best to market yourself. Having one can enlarge the number of opportunities available to you as a performer and accelerate your career and income level much faster than you could on your own. But it's important to remember that an agent is not a magical ticket to a life of sudden fame and fortune. In fact, an agent is unlikely to be interested in you unless your career is already under way to some degree.

Agents need to see at least some economic activity that they can enlarge upon and monetize. That means that you need to do the initial work of finding an audience and promoting yourself. An agent can fan the flames of your career, but you've got to provide that initial spark.

HOW TO FIND AN AGENT

If you're serious about mastering your craft as a performer, working hard to pursue opportunities, and doing your best to maintain a positive, professional attitude, that makes you very desirable to an agent. While the supply of people with ambitions in the performing arts is large, it is not infinite. Agents need new clients to keep their work going. And agents want to work with good people just as much as you do. So don't fall for the trap of thinking that you have to work with the first agent you meet or the first one who approaches you. Take the time to find the right fit.

The best place to start is with your fellow performers, both those who are at the same stage as you in your career and those who are farther down the road. Find people whose careers you admire and look to see who represents them. Take a look at each agent's roster of talent. If you see somebody you know, ask her what it's like to work with that person, and if you like what you hear, then don't be afraid about contacting the agent. (See below for tips on approaching an agent.)

And don't dismiss networking events that are explicitly designed to pair up agents with new talent or that are designed to help performers develop their careers. In the early stages of your career, keep an open mind about every opportunity to meet people and learn.

WHAT TO LOOK FOR IN AN AGENT

Like any profession, the performing arts world is a community as much as it is a mass of people trying to make a living. When looking for an agent, seek out people who care about being a contributing member of that community. The work of an agent depends heavily on personal connections, so look for people who have a big network and whose work is happily integrated into their full life. Having an agent who just sees his work as a 9 to 5 obligation isn't going to get you nearly as far as somebody who derives real pleasure and meaning from his work. Look for somebody who has a passionate concern for your art form, who gets excited about helping bring great art into the world.

HOW TO APPROACH AN AGENT

An agent wants to work with people who are dedicated to their work and enthusiastic about their career. As we've said elsewhere, in a field crowded with talented prospects, attitude makes a big difference. It's something you can control, and it can really give you an edge.

Don't worry about having the perfect head shots, bio, and work portfolio. Those are all things that a good agent can help you develop. But not having these things at all sends the wrong signal. Do your best to work up these things on your own. It shows that you're serious.

The same goes for having a sense of your personal brand—what you do well and where you might fit into your field. An agent can help you refine this, but the more information you can give on this front, the easier it will be for the agent to picture how to market you and what contacts might want to work with you. When the all-male vocal quartet New York Polyphony (see Chapter 7) first started working with the classical music talent agency Opus 3, the agency had trouble differentiating the group from Chanticleer, another all-male vocal ensemble. The members of New York Polyphony had already established on their own that their repertoire was more classical and more devoted to early music than Chanticleer's. They even described themselves as a "vocal string quartet," in contrast to Chanticleer's description of itself as an "orchestra of voices." Having a clearly differentiated brand ready to go made it much easier for Opus 3 to promote New York Polyphony in the United States and around the world.

HOW TO WORK WITH AN AGENT

Remember that having an agent is, above all, a personal relationship. Just as with a friend, hopefully you have somebody with whom you can have a positive, long-term connection. This will make it easier to work together over time, and it will make the agent's work a pleasure rather than a chore. That's something you'll both be grateful for.

Treat your agent as a colleague, not as somebody providing a service. If you feel that your agent isn't living up to his end of the bargain, don't let your relationship get gummed up with negative emotions like resentment or a sense of entitlement. It's okay to be assertive about your needs, but don't give in to negativity. And if you feel your agent is doing great work and helping you, don't be afraid to let him know.

Be open and authentic with your agent. If something is happening in your life that might prevent you from pursuing a job—like a sick relative, a medical issue, or anything else that might seem personal—don't be afraid to let your agent know about it. This can stop her from jumping on an opportunity that you might not be able to pursue. The same goes for challenges in the moment. Always do your best to be prepared, but if you're in a jam and need something at the last second, don't be embarrassed to pick up the phone and call for help. Your agent wants you to succeed just as much as you do! In order to get the most from any relationship, the other person has to know what your needs and desires are. So open up and don't be afraid to make a real connection.

★ ★ ANGELA'S STORY ★ ★

by William F. Baker

Since the material elsewhere in this chapter is perhaps most useful to actors, I thought it would be worthwhile to tell the story of my daughter's journey in the world of live theater in New York City.

This is a true story. There are many amazing, successful actors on Broadway and in films who have made it. But we rarely hear of the great percentage of those who didn't and decided to move on to other careers. This is one part of the business of the performing arts that we have not gone into elsewhere in the book. It is maybe not a happy story for a person seeking a career as an actor or as any kind of performer, but it is still one we can learn from.

It was 20 years ago when my daughter Angela, after having performed in a number of local high school and church plays, announced she wanted to go to Broadway! I was running a large public broadcasting station in New York and had many friends in the management and ownership of Broadway theaters, so I thought I knew what she was in for. It turns out I was only slightly knowledgeable. I knew it would be hard, but I didn't expect it to be as hard as it turned out to be.

With the full support of me and my wife, Angela applied to and got into one of the top New York universities with a world-famous theater program. I attended most of her public performances there and watched her grow while always wondering about her future. I knew this school was excellent and saw her grow in skill and confidence, but I also saw some pretty strange, experimental plays during that period. I'll never forget the one with a naked girl in a cage groaning for a half hour—that was it! I wasn't too sure about the value of that.

After her top-of-class graduation (and $250,000 in tuition money), I wondered what was next and offered to help. I explained that I knew most of the theater owners and producers, which meant that at least they'd be willing to take a look at her. My daughter said she was grateful for my intention, but she wanted to do it on her own, so "no, thanks."

Next came the endless auditions and literally hundreds of rejections. At the start, there were a few successes here and there, but nothing major. It was enough, however, for her to start building a résumé and get into the theater and film unions, which gave her the possibility of major success.

Keeping a roof over her head and food on the table was very expensive in New York City, so she did what most actors do and waited tables. It turns out she was very good at it and did quite well economically. But she hated the work, and it wasn't sustainable in the long term.

Meanwhile, it was a year or two more of rejections until she landed a spot in a new Broadway repertory company in which she had small non-speaking roles. She got to work regularly with and befriend many major name actors. They were often very kind and caring people. And they were eager to help her. Far from being cutthroat, the theater community turned out to be very close-knit and sometimes selfless. The problem for Angela, who was clearly talented, was that there seemed to be very few major parts for 20-something actors. The stars were all in their 40s and 50s, even older.

So even after joining the unions and getting a place in a repertory company, it was still waitressing and the immense frustration of not doing what she was trained to do.

Finally, after about five years, she came to me and said she could use my help. I was delighted to hear that and was sure I could pull some strings and make something happen. I fired both barrels and called all my friends in the business and asked for their help. Surprisingly the usual comment was, "I'm in no position to help your daughter." I was aghast. These guys owned the theaters or were the producers of the plays! "Couldn't they do something?" I thought. In many ways, though, I was happy to hear that they couldn't do anything. The acting world, despite rumors to the contrary, turned out to truly be a meritocracy. But that alignment of talent and opportunity continued to elude my daughter. Every director has something specific in his own mind and relentlessly seeks somebody with the look and feel that matches that vision. And that's okay. After all, it's art, not science! But it didn't make it easier for Angela.

Despite the challenges, she kept chalking up credits and getting her name in *Playbill*. After a while, she had a real résumé, but still no financial success! So even with professional credits, it was back to the restaurant, night after night.

After seven years, she did what she said she'd never do, and she threw in the towel.

My wife and I were in fact happy. We had seen up close what a hard and brutal life an actor faces, and we were not sure we wanted that for our daughter. She had grown a great deal personally in the process. She was beautiful, had poise, and was very intelligent and fun to be around. She would have a bright future in whatever career she chose.

Her next career was following my wife into psychiatric nursing. She became a nurse practitioner. At her first job at Memorial Sloan Kettering Cancer Center, she said she was worried about being a great nurse in such a high-stress, high-demand environment. I told her that she might not be a great nurse yet, but she was a great actress, "so act like a great nurse!" As a nurse, she has gone on to great success. She loves her work and is beloved by her patients, who are as great and grateful an audience as she could ever have hoped for.

★ ★ **KEYNOTES** ★ ★

Questions to Ask Yourself
- What is my attitude toward auditions? Am I afraid of them? Do I fear them as judgments of my self-worth?
- Do I have a way of supporting myself while I build up steam in my career?

Tips

- The personal relationships made in the theater community (and all communities of performers) are critical, and often friends who are actors and directors are the ones who will make your career possible. When you rub shoulders with your peers, famous and obscure, don't be afraid to say hello.

- Look for agents who are passionate about your art form and who are enmeshed in the artistic community. Do they show up to events outside of working hours? Do other actors and agents know them and speak about them positively?

Exercises

- Search your community for organizations or regularly held events that are designed to bring new talent together with agents, and attend one.

- Make a list of five to ten performing artists whose careers you admire. They can be anybody from people in your community to superstars. Find out who their agents are, and see who else those agents represent. Do you know any or can you get an introduction to one? Is there a common element to their careers?

THE GRADUATION SPEECH

You don't have to read this book from start to finish to get the full benefit from it, but we couldn't resist penning some proper closing remarks. This book started as a class, and this chapter is a version of the presentation given during the last class session each spring, just weeks before the students start their post-college careers. It's something to send them, and now you, off on a good note.

———

We have seen that the serious American performing arts industry is a complex creature to understand. It's highly fragmented, relatively small economically, buffeted by changes in technology, and shrinking. Where does that leave a talented performer?

When we look at the future of the performing arts, we see opportunity.

The preceding chapters showed that others have "found the opening (opportunity) and gone through it." Business creativity is different from performance creativity. You may strive for perfection in performance, but to be creative in business you need not achieve perfection—you just need to create something sufficiently different that will attract attention and create demand.

For starters, you can take advantage of the Internet by producing and marketing sample performances online like Petra Conti did (Chapter 4). This begins to build your brand and hopefully an audience that might pay to see performances. Get out there and perform in venues that have been anathema to others, just to be visible and unique. It's okay to be afraid!

There's a wonderful conservatory-trained pianist, Andrew Shapiro, in New York who "has his eyes on the fries." That is, he took up playing the piano at a McDonald's in downtown Manhattan in 2004. He gets paid for the gig and loves doing it. He meets people from all around the world and gets high praise for his performance. For McDonald's, Andrew increases sales and brings in new customers. The unusual venue has attracted media attention, and Andrew has received and accepted offers to play in places as far away as Poland. He is talked about and has built a following of people who like his work. Andrew's career is proof that opportunity can be found anywhere.[1]

There are many ways to make it, and you'll have to work just as hard at promoting yourself, running your business, and raising money as you do at your art, at least at the beginning. Just about every artist we know who has made it tells us that. Of course, there are exceptions. If the stars align themselves just right, you might find yourself walking right into a successful orchestra or dance company or getting a spot on Broadway. But that's clearly the exception. More than likely, you will experience slow, uneven, uphill progress toward your goal.

No matter what, you'll have to understand the business you are in to make your career pay off. Mickey Mantle was quoted as saying, "It's unbelievable how much you don't know about the game you've been playing all your life." Mickey had the advantage of playing baseball with team management people taking care of the business. If you just can't handle the business, you'll need a partner or friend, or you may have to work for an organization that will handle the business issues as the Yankees did for Mickey. Sure, it's getting harder to find traditional arts companies that are growing and hiring these days. In the beginning, the responsibility will likely fall on your shoulders. But don't worry. You can do it! You can see from what we've written that it's not impossible.

★ ★ KEYNOTES ★ ★

For this final round of Keynotes, we think you've earned the right to forgo any questions and exercises. Instead, take these final tips. If we had to reduce everything we've written down into a *secret sauce*, here it is. When you're stuck, or when you're going so fast that you don't know what the next right move is, one of the following 14 ideas will not steer you wrong.

1. **Be authentic.** Don't try to do something that doesn't come from deep within you, and don't try to fake it. If you don't know something and are nervous, say so—people appreciate honesty. Conversely, if you believe deeply that something should be done differently because all your knowledge and training tells you so, speak up!

2. **Ask for help.** We know that you are likely in a strange environment when starting a business or asking for money, but there are many people who will be impressed with your artistic gifts and be willing to help. *You just have to ask.* You can enlist friends for legal help or accounting knowledge right from the start.

3. **Offer help.** Use your gifts to help others. You'd be surprised how being a "giver" pays back and increases the satisfaction you can get from the nonartistic part of your work.

4. **Start small.** Don't take big economic risks early on that could sink your enterprise while it's still in the dock.

5. **Do something crazy.** Play or dance in an unusual venue. Get some friends to help make a creative video that gets attention on YouTube, where you can direct folks to your work. As long as you are not taking on undue financial risks at the start, let your imagination be the only thing that limits your ambition.

6. **Network.** And do it in every way and using all media, including the phone, Internet, and in person.

7. **Ask for advice.** This complement to networking is going to others who have succeeded in the arts or business and getting their advice. Many more are willing to help than you'd imagine, especially those who are retired or near the end of their careers.

8. **Develop a business plan.** The plan need not be complex, but it will help organize your thoughts, give you direction, and make it easier for you to explain what you are trying to do and what you need.

9. **Find a niche.** Look for a need that you can fill or a type of work that you can specialize in. It needn't be completely unique; it could be something that has already been done but in another place, or it could be something that was tried and failed elsewhere, but you could do it better or you are in the right place at the right time. The key here is a combination of trial and error. You won't be able to find your niche by thinking really hard about it in isolation. You've got to get out there and get your hands dirty.

10. **Expect the unexpected in your career path.** Your path to mastery of your art was linear; your career path will not be. The working world is full of chance opportunities and unex-

pected turns. There are no teachers and no grades. It will be scary, but above all it will be an adventure.

11. **Realize that you are in the people business whether you're a performer or a manager.** Cultivate your relationships. Attend to the mindset and the intangible needs of those around you at work and at play. When your colleagues or employees do a good job, tell them! When they don't, tell them that too, but respectfully. Remember that no one is only the function she does. People are complex, wonderful creatures. Every working relationship is first and foremost a relationship.

12. **Know when to back away.** If disagreements arise in your organization, you may need to back away from your struggle to find the right answer to the problem. If you and your colleagues can't agree on the right answer, consider whether you need to ask different questions.

13. **Beware of burnout.** Take a cue from Peter Gelb, whose employment contract actually stipulates that he has to be available 24/7. As general manager of the Metropolitan Opera, he is as vulnerable to burnout as anyone. He avoids it in two ways: by staying close to the mission of his organization, and by staying proactive.

    Gelb makes a point of showing up for at least some of each night's performance. He says it reinforces that the excitement, glamour, and trascendent qualities of opera are why he keeps showing up every day. His advice is echoed by almost all the other administrators and artists we interviewed. Stay close to the art, and you are sure not to lose stamina for your work.

14. **Start.** Get going! Stop thinking and talking about it (and even reading about it)—get moving. Time is wasting!

Finally, what makes all this effort worth it? The answer is suggested by this quotation from Plato, carved into the lobby wall of Cleveland's Severance Hall. It's about music, but we think it captures the essence of those rare, transcendent moments in all the performing arts:

Music is a moral law. It gives a soul to the universe, wings to the mind, flight to the imagination, a charm to gaiety and life to everything. It's the essence of order and leads to all that is good, just and beautiful.

ACKNOWLEDGMENTS

FROM WILLIAM F. BAKER

Special thanks to Deans Robert Grimes, Donna Rapaccioli, and James Hennessy at Fordham University, and to Katherine Gerston at The Juilliard School for their guidance and support for my classes. Karen Hayward, who assisted in organizing and teaching the course "Understanding the Profession: The Performing Arts in the 21st Century." David Horn at WNET, who was always willing to help. Laura Walker at WNYC, who is a real pro in the business. Ed Reilly at the American Management Association, who gave this unusual book his full support. Provosts Stephen Freedman at Fordham and Ara Guzelimian at Juilliard, who fully supported my work. The many wonderful faculty members at Juilliard, especially Bärli Nugent, who were always there for us. Andrew Gundlach, who gave our students big-time business advice, and Tim Domini, who helped them read financial statements. Martin Kagan, who understands the business like nobody we know and eagerly shares his knowledge. Eric Hurtig, a key member of the Schwartz Center team, who was always at the ready to fill in the blanks. Greg Sandow, a Juilliard colleague who had tremendous insight.

Barrett Hipes and Courtney Blackwell, for their leadership in helping artist-entrepreneurs. And Larry Lynn, for doing an amazing job, as ever.

FROM WARREN C. GIBSON

Thanks to my wife, Merrilee, for her support. It's a special pleasure to work with Bill Baker, a dear friend of more than 60 years.

FROM EVAN LEATHERWOOD

Special thanks to my two coauthors for making this book happen in the first place and for their wisdom, patience, and support. Andrew Yang, for being by my side every step of the way. Our editor, Stephen S. Power, for insight and meticulous guidance. The staff of the New York Society Library, for providing a place of comfort, scholarship, and silence. The talented students of "Understanding the Profession: The Performing Arts in the 21st Century," for their discipline, really great questions, and mischief. Eric Hurtig, for his bottomless well of good ideas and hard data. Carolyn Velazquez-Atis and the rest of the Fordham crew, for making me feel at home. Jeannemarie Baker, for her upbeat attitude. My brilliant, patient, and willing interview subjects: Rachel S. Moore, Daniel Talbott, Claire Chase, Peter Gelb, Max Hodges, Sir Clive Gillinson, Christopher Dylan Herbert, Loni Landon and Gregory Dolbashian, Alex Lipowski, Dustin Flores and Paula Poeta, and Diane Wittry. Neil Fiore and the other Neal for handing me the right tools in the nick of time. Barrett Hipes and the Juilliard career services office, for giving us the right name just when we needed it. Alexa and Marc Suskin, for their unflagging support. The boys and girls of CRUX Climbing, for giving me a place to let go of my worries. Barbara Slifka and Bernard L. Schwartz, for making it all possible. My fellows, for keeping me focused on progress, not perfection. My family, of course. And to all the people I forgot to mention, thank you.

NOTES

Chapter 2: Struggles and Triumphs of Western Musicians

1. George R. Marek, *Beethoven: Biography of a Genius* (New York: Funk & Wagnalls, 1969), pp. 93, 94.
2. http://www.beethoven-haus-bonn.de/sixcms/list.php?page=museum_internetausstellung_seiten_en&sv[internetausstellung.id]=31561&skip=9, accessed July 2014.
3. Ibid.
4. Jim Whiting, *The Life and Times of Giuseppe Verdi* (Hockesin, DE: Mitchell Lane Publishers, 2005), p. 40.
5. Peter Davis, *The American Opera Singer: The Lives and Adventures of America's Great Singers in Opera and in Concert from 1825 to the Present* (New York: Doubleday, 1997), p. 134.
6. Ibid.
7. Ibid., p. 135.
8. Ibid., p. 129.
9. "Bubbles—Beverly Sills," www.diarci.com/2012/12/10/bubbles-beverly-sills/, accessed May 1, 2015.
10. Ibid.
11. William F. Baker and Michael O'Malley, *Leading with Kindness* (New York: Amacom, 2008).
12. Anthony Tommasini, "Beverly Sills, Acclaimed Soprano, Dies at 78," *New York Times*, July 2, 2007, accessed May 20, 2009.
13. Anthony Tommasini, "Lessons in a Year of Crises," *New York Times*, January 8, 2014.

Chapter 3: The Performing Arts as an Industry

1. Michael Cooper, "Met Opera Tax Filing Reveals Pay for Gelb," *New York Times*, June 16, 2014, http://www.nytimes.com/2014/06/17/arts/music/met-opera-tax-filing-reveals-pay-for-gelb-and-angers-unions.html?_r=0, accessed May 28, 2015.
2. Ibid.
3. U.S. Census Bureau, "Industry Statistics Portal, Business Data from the U.S. Census Bureau, 2012 NAICS 71—Arts, Entertainment, and Recreation," http://www.census.gov/econ/isp/sampler.php?naicscode=71&naicslevel=2, accessed June 1, 2015).

4. Ibid.
5. "Giving USA 2011" (Chicago: Indiana University Center on Philanthropy, 2011), www.givingusa.org, accessed June 1, 2015.
6. U.S. Census Bureau.
7. U.S. Department of Labor, "May 2014 National Industry-Specific Occupational Employment and Wage Estimates, NAICS 711100—Performing Arts Companies," http://www.bls.gov/oes/current/naics4_711100.htm#27-0000, accessed June 1, 2015.

Chapter 4: The Digital Revolution and the Performing Arts

1. Louis Menand, "Crooner in Rights Spat: Are Copyright Laws Too Strict?" *New Yorker*, October 20, 2014.
2. Luis Cabral, *The Economics of Entertainment and Sports: Concepts and Cases* (unpublished academic paper, 2015).
3. Richard Campbell et al., *Media and Culture: An Introduction to Mass Communication,* ninth edition (New York: Bedford/St. Martin's Press, 2004).
4. Martha Mendoza, "How Facebook Likes Get Bought and Sold," *Huffington Post*, January 5, 2014, http://www.huffingtonpost.com/2014/01/05/buy-facebook-likes_n_4544800.html, accessed June 5, 2015.
5. Michael Tilson Thomas, TED 2012.

Chapter 5: Reading and Understanding Financial Statements

1. Johann Wolfgang von Goethe, "Wilhelm Meister's Apprenticeship," [1795] trans. in Eric Blackall, ed., *Goethe: The Collected Works*, vol. 9 (Princeton, NJ: Princeton University Press, 1995).
2. "Michael Tilson Thomas, Worth Every Penny," *Los Angeles Times*, December 14, 2008.

Chapter 6: Essential Lessons from the Great Managers

1. Peter Gelb in email correspondence with Evan Leatherwood, December 14, 2014.
2. Nicole Gelinas, "The Met's Fiscal Tragicomedy, When the 1% Stop Giving," *New York Times*, August 4, 2014.
3. Peter Gelb in conversation with William F. Baker and Evan Leatherwood, March 25, 2013, on the campus of the Juilliard School, New York City.
4. Anita Elberse and Crissy Perez, "The Metropolitan Opera (A)," Harvard Business School Study 9-509-033, March 23, 2009 (Boston: Harvard Business School Publishing), p. 12, Exhibit 2D.
5. Ibid., p. 4.
6. "New York's Met Faces 'Social Rejection of Opera,'" http://www.dw.de/new-yorks-met-faces-social-rejection-of-opera/a-17595752, accessed August 31, 2014.
7. Fred Plotkin, "What's Ailing Opera in America?" http://www.wqxr.org/story/174092-whats-ailing-opera-america/, December 2, 2011, accessed August 20, 2014.
8. Elizabeth Maupin, "Orlando Opera to File for Bankruptcy," *Orlando Sentinel*, http://articles.orlandosentinel.com/2009-04-28/news/Opera_1_orlando-opera-united-arts-sabol, April 28, 2008.
9. Bettina A. Norton, "Opera Lovers Stunned by Opera Boston's Closing," *Boston Musical Intelligencer*, http://www.classical-scene.com/2011/12/23/opera-boston-closing/, December 23, 2011, accessed August 20, 2014.
10. James B. Stewart, "A Ransacked Endowment at New York City Opera," *New York Times*, http://www.nytimes.com/2013/10/12/business/ransacking-the-endowment-at-new-york-city-opera.html?pagewanted=all&pagewanted=print, October 11, 2013, accessed August 28, 2014.

11. Peter Gelb in email correspondence with William F. Baker, December 8, 2014.
12. Peter Gelb in conversation with William F. Baker, March 26, 2014, on the campus of the Juilliard School, New York City.
13. Ibid.
14. "The Met: Live in HD Fact Sheet 2012–13" (New York: The Metropolitan Opera, August 20, 2012).
15. Ibid.
16. Ibid.
17. Peter Gelb and Matthew Dobkin in email correspondence with William F. Baker, April 3, 2015.
18. Ibid.
19. Gelb in conversation with Baker, March 26, 2014.
20. Ibid.
21. Ibid.
22. Michael Cooper, "In Surprise Finale at Metropolitan Opera's Labor Talks, Both Sides Agree to Cuts," *New York Times*, August 18, 2014.
23. Robin Pogrebin, "Metropolitan Opera Receives $30 Million Gift," *New York Times*, http://www.nytimes.com/2010/03/27/arts/music/27gift.html, March 26, 2010, accessed August 19, 2014; Gelb and Dobkin in email correspondence with Baker and Leatherwood, April 3, 2015.
24. Gelb in conversation with Baker, March 26, 2014.
25. Ibid.
26. Sir Clive Gillinson in conversation with William F. Baker and Evan Leatherwood, February 26, 2014, on the campus of the Juilliard School, New York City.
27. "Behind Bars: Music at Sing Sing," video posted by Carnegie Hall: Weill Music Institute, https://www.youtube.com/watch?v=TBYRMgPny-k, viewed April 14, 2015.
28. Gillinson in conversation with Baker and Leatherwood, February 26, 2014.
29. "Behind Bars: Music at Sing Sing."
30. Meredith "Max" Hodges, live presentation, January 22, 2014, on the campus of the Juilliard School, New York City.
31. Ibid.
32. Ibid.
33. Ibid.
34. Ibid.
35. Ibid.
36. Ibid.
37. Ibid.
38. Ibid.
39. Ibid.
40. Ibid.
41. Annual revenues for the Paul Taylor Dance Company: 2011—$6.7 million, 2010—$6.3 million, 2009—$5.2 million, 2008—$9.1 million. Source: U.S. Department of the Treasury, Internal Revenue Service, Form 990 for the Paul Taylor Dance Company, accessed from www.guidestar.org February 15, 2014.
42. Max Hodges in email correspondence with Evan Leatherwood, March 10, 2014.
43. Hodges, live presentation, January 22, 2014.
44. Ibid.
45. "Tell Me, What Is It You Plan to Do with Your One Wild and Precious Life?" from *Portrait Project* by Tony Deifell, http://www.hbs.edu/PortraitProject/2010/HodgesMax.html, accessed September 16, 2014.
46. Hodges in email correspondence with Leatherwood, March 10, 2014.
47. Rachel S. Moore interviewed by Evan Leatherwood at the offices of American Ballet Theatre, New York City, May 2, 2014.
48. Ibid.

49. Rachel S. Moore in conversation with William F. Baker and Evan Leatherwood, April 23, 2014, on the campus of the Juilliard School, New York City.

50. Ibid.

51. "United States Congress Honors American Ballet Theatre," May 5, 2006, Ballet Theatre Foundation, http://www.abt.org/insideabt/news_display.asp?News_ID=160, accessed November 13, 2014.

52. Moore interviewed by Evan Leatherwood at the offices of American Ballet Theartre, New York City, on May 2, 2014.

53. Ibid.

54. Rachel S. Moore in email correspondence with Evan Leatherwood, March 31, 2015.

55. Moore interviewed by Leatherwood, May 2, 2014.

56. Ibid.

57. Ibid.

58. Jeanne Sahadi, "Top Ten Millionaire Counties," CNNMoney.com, http://biz.yahoo.com/special/trophyhome06_article1.html, accessed November 13, 2014.

59. Moore interviewed by Leatherwood, May 2, 2014.

60. Ibid.

Chapter 7: Essential Lessons from the Artist-Entrepreneurs

1. Claire Chase interviewed by Evan Leatherwood, February 15, 2012, on the campus of the Juilliard School, New York City.

2. Claire Chase interviewed by Evan Leatherwood, Autumn 2013, at ICEHaus, headquarters of the International Contemporary Ensemble—New York Chapter in Brooklyn, New York.

3. "The Ensemble Modern's History," https://www.ensemble-modern.com/en/ensemble_modern/history, accessed April 10, 2015.

4. Chase interviewed by Leatherwood, Autumn 2013.

5. Ibid.

6. Chase interviewed by Leatherwood, February 15, 2012.

7. "International Contemporary Ensemble Foundation," Andrew W. Mellon Foundation Grants database, http://mellon.org/grants/grants-database/grants/international-contemporary-ensemble-foundation-inc/41000660/, accessed October 14, 2014.

8. "ICElab a New Model for New Music," http://iceorg/icelab, accessed October 14, 2014.

9. Chase interviewed by Leatherwood, February 15, 2012.

10. Diane Wittry, live presentation, January 29, 2014, on the campus of the Juilliard School, New York City.

11. Daniel Talbott in Los Angeles interviewed by Evan Leatherwood in New York via phone, March 16, 2015.

12. Ibid.

13. All information about AEA requirements from Actors' Equity Association, "Basic Showcase Code" (New York: AEA, January 2006), www.actorsequity.org, accessed April 10, 2015.

14. Talbott interviewed by Leatherwood, March 16, 2015.

15. Ibid.

16. All information about AEA requirements from Actors' Equity Association, "Basic Showcase Code" (New York: AEA, January 2006), www.actorsequity.org, accessed April 10, 2015.

17. Talbott interviewed by Leatherwood, March 16, 2015.

18. Christopher Dylan Herbert interviewed by Evan Leatherwood in Brooklyn, New York, September 9, 2014.

19. Ibid.

20. Ibid.

21. Ibid.

22. Ibid.

23. Ibid.

24. High figure of about $30 based on rates posted online in November 2014 per class for Gibney Dance ($17 for a pro ballet class), Alvin Ailey Extension ($32 per class), Paul Taylor Dance Company ($14 to $16 per class), and New York City Ballet ($22 per class).

25. Assuming that you took five classes per week at the lowest available rate ($14 at Paul Taylor Dance Company), that would come out to $280 per month.

26. Miriam Kreinin Souccar, "Workin' Hard for the Money: Dancers on Poverty Line," *Crain's New York Business*, http://www.crainsnewyork.com/article/20120227/ARTS/120229923/-workin-hard-for-the-money-dancers-on-poverty-line, February 17, 2012, accessed April 14, 2014.

27. Loni Landon and Gregory Dolbashian interviewed by Evan Leatherwood, October 1, 2013, at Fordham University's Lincoln Center Campus, New York City.

28. Ibid.

29. Ibid.

30. Ibid.

31. Elena Hecht, "The Playground" in "2013 25 to Watch," *Dance Magazine*, http://www.dance-magazine.com/issues/january-2013/2013-25-to-watch, January 2013, accessed April 14, 2015.

32. Alex Lipowski interviewed by Evan Leatherwood, September 24, 2012, at the Talea Ensemble studio, Long Island City, New York.

33. Ibid.

34. Ibid.

35. Ibid.

Chapter 9: Auditions, Agents, and Angela's Story

1. Paula Poeta and Dustin Flores interviewed by Evan Leatherwood and William F. Baker on the campus of the Juilliard School, February 11, 2015.

2. Gavin Bond, "The X-Files 1993/2002," *Entertainment Weekly*, October 25–November 1, 2013.

Chapter 10: The Graduation Speech

1. Kim Nowacki, "McDonald's Pianist: I'm Loving It," *WQXR Blog*, December 23, 2011, accessed July 2, 2015.

INDEX

ABOUT THE AUTHORS

William F. Baker, Ph.D., is an award-winning producer and media executive. He is the Claudio Aquaviva Professor of Education at Fordham University, where he directs the Bernard L. Schwartz Center for Media, Public Policy, and Education. He is also president emeritus of WNET, New York's flagship PBS station. Since 2010, he has taught "Understanding the Profession: The Performing Arts in the 21st Century" to a select group of students at the Juilliard School and at Fordham University.

Warren C. Gibson, Ph.D., is a professional engineer and retired cofounder of CSA Engineering, Inc., Mountain View, California, a firm specializing in vibration suppression and precision motion control. He is also an economist and currently lectures on that subject at San Jose State University. Bill and Warren grew up together in the 1950s in Cleveland.

Evan Leatherwood is a journalist, a speaker, and a Slifka Fellow at the Bernard L. Schwartz Center for Media, Public Policy, and Education at Fordham University. His work has appeared on public television and in the *Nation*, the *Columbia Journalism Review*, the *New York Daily News*, and other publications of note. He is a graduate of Yale University and lives in New York City.